ASMARA

AFRICA'S SECRET MODERNIST CITY

ምስጢር ህንጻታት አስመራ

ASMARA

AFRICA'S SECRET MODERNIST CITY

Edward Denison
Guang Yu Ren
Naigzy Gebremedhin

MERRELL
LONDON · NEW YORK

First published 2003 by Merrell Publishers Limited

Head office:
42 Southwark Street
London SE1 1UN

New York office:
49 West 24th Street
New York, NY 10010

www.merrellpublishers.com

Publisher Hugh Merrell
Editorial Director Julian Honer
US Director Joan Brookbank
Sales and Marketing Director Emilie Nangle
Managing Editor Anthea Snow
Editor Sam Wythe
Design Manager Kate Ward
Production Manager Michelle Draycott
Editorial and Production Assistant Emily Sanders

British Library Cataloguing-in-Publication Data:
Edward Denison
Asmara : Africa's secret modernist city
1.Modern movement (Architecture) – Eritrea – Asmara
2.Asmara (Eritrea) – Buildings, structures, etc.
I.Title II.Ren, Guang Yu III.Gebremedhin, Naigzy
720.9'635

ISBN 1 85894 209 8

Produced by Merrell Publishers Limited
Edited by Sarah Yates with Laura Hicks
Designed by Karen Wilks
Indexed by Laura Hicks
Printed and bound in Italy

Note on the text: original building names are given in Italian where known and
where the Italian names are not subject to variation.

Page 2: Selam Hotel, 1937 (see pages 156–58); Page 10: Interior of an apartment
building on the site of the Unione Militare (see page 211); Pages 14–15: Silicon
factory, 1938 (see pages 146–47); Pages 84–85: Workshop and service station,
1938 (see pages 150–51); Pages 86–87: Government office, 1889–95 (see page 89);
Pages 120–21: Ministry of Tourism, approximately 1938 (see page 154); Pages
200–01: Municipality, 1951–71 (see pages 202–04); Pages 220–21: Shops and
apartments, 1956 (see page 227)

The Coptic script shown on page 1 translates as "Asmara's secret buildings".

CONTENTS

ACKNOWLEDGEMENTS

CONTRIBUTORS

Gabriel Tseggai is currently Director of the Planning Division at the Department of Urban Development in Eritrea. He has worked in the department since its inception in 1991, since when he has gained a Master's degree in Urban Development and Design at the University of New South Wales, Sydney, Australia. In his current post he has been involved in the preparation of plans for several towns in Eritrea (although not those for Asmara). He also has a personal interest in Asmara, as he was born and grew up in the city, and has witnessed the many changes in its more recent history. He has presented and had published papers on the future development of Asmara, and believes that there is much to learn from the design, history and unique social environment of the city.

Professor Peppo Brivio is Senior Adviser to the Cultural Assets Rehabilitation Project of Eritrea (CARP). With architectural experience spanning seven decades, he could be considered one of the world's leading authorities on the history of Modernist architecture. He began practising architecture in the 1940s and by 1955 had established his own practice, which he directed for twenty-five years. In 1969 he combined practice with teaching when he became Professor of Contemporary History of Architecture in the School of Architecture at Geneva University; later he also ran the university's architectural practice, until 1989. In 1991 he was awarded an honorary Professorship at the same institution. In the 1990s he became involved in the preservation of Asmara, and was selected as Senior Adviser to CARP in 2000.

The conception and completion of this book has resulted from an intensely collaborative and inclusive process spanning many years and including a great many devoted and impassioned individuals and organizations. If there were a single name under which the greatest number of contributors might willingly be represented, it would be that of CARP. This book, therefore, should be seen as a product of the much wider endeavours of CARP and those involved with it, and it is to those many people that most credit must be paid.

In the light of the gratitude that the authors owe to so many individuals who have contributed to this book, regrettably there is not enough space in which to thank everyone adequately. However, their efforts have most certainly been profoundly appreciated. Our thanks must first go to those who facilitated CARP's development into a feasible, largely autonomous and financially viable body. Many thanks also go to Mayor Semere Russom, who allowed access to the municipality's archives for the very first time, without which this book would not have been conceivable, and to the many municipality staff who generously provided so much assistance, and with whom CARP is proud to have such a productive and valued relationship.

There are also many individuals who have worked so hard since Eritrea became independent to raise awareness about Asmara around the world – this book has been created from the sound foundation you established. Among these many committed individuals stand Dawit Debessay, Nadine Bolle and, not least,

Professor Peppo Brivio, for his guidance, experience and ubiquitous insights. We are indebted to those who so generously and willingly provided invaluable materials from their precious collections, including Brother Ezio at the Pavoni Library and the ever-willing Vahe Koroghlian. Thank you also to Gabriel Tseggai for his enlightened contributions, guided tours of Asmara's 'underbelly', and profound friendship; to Amanuel Ghebray and Tsehainesh Tekle; to all those working closely with CARP for their significant contributions: Mebrahtu Abraham, for his seemingly boundless knowledge of, and enthusiasm for, Eritrean history; Berhane Mehari, for always helping out whenever help was needed; Alemseged Tesfai, for valuable advice and support; and of course Worede, Hailemicheal, Dawit, Tebe, Lateselassie, Negusse and Kudusan; to Dr Negusse Araya and all the staff at the British Council for their constant professionalism, amity and unmitigated support; to His Excellency Mike Murray, the British Ambassador to Eritrea, his wife Birgitta, and the staff at the British Embassy; to Wieni Dessalegn; to those outside Eritrea whose constant support, input and presence were crucial – Giulia Barrera, Carla Ghezzi, Francesco and the staff in the IsIAO Library, Francesca Locatelli, Silvana Palma, Paolo Scattoni, Maria Pina Di Simone, Stefania Scipioni, Ren He Tian, Ho Ji Xin, Eleanor and John Denison not least for their reams of translation of Italian and seemingly endless proof-reading, Moges Naigzy, Donica and, of course, Noah; to the many professionals and scholars around the world without whose contributions this book would have been an irrelevance – Arlene Fleming, Woldai Futur, Eritros Abraham for your valuable assistance, Mia Fuller,

Shumondi Bereket, Magnus Treiber, Ladislao Ricci, Zambia, Guido and Paola at the Italian School, Beth Hatherall, and especially to our dearest friends Semira, Sallahadin and Heden; to all the generous owners of the properties that appear in this book; Aregahegn, Renee, Yohannes and Tsion; and to Hugh Merrell, Julian Honer and all the staff at Merrell Publishers for accepting this project so enthusiastically and completing it so professionally: Anthea Snow for your scrupulous input and guidance; Kate Ward and Michelle Draycott for your kind dedication and professionalism; Karen Wilks for your excellent design and attention to detail; and Sarah Yates and Laura Hicks for your exceptional editing. Above all, your immeasurab patience and commitment to seeing this project through to its most successful conclusion deserves a special mention – thank you all.

Finally, it remains for us to thank the innumerable individuals who contributed to this book in ways that perhaps they were even unaware of and can best be described as 'all Eritreans'. This book is about you and for you, and may it do justice to your home and the bright future that you strive for and so deserve. Rather than an end in itself, this book marks the end of the beginning from which much essential work must follow.

THE CULTURAL ASSETS REHABILITATION PROJECT (CARP)

The Cultural Assets Rehabilitation Project (CARP) is an initiative of the Eritrean Government and the people of Eritrea in recognition of the importance of preserving all aspects of the nation's cultural heritage as an affirmation of its distinctive spiritual, material, intellectual and emotional attributes.

Preservation of the cultural heritage is being undertaken through four main activities: conservation of monuments and heritage assets; conservation of the built environment of Eritrean towns and cities, including Asmara and Massawa; support for living culture, including poetry, dance and folklore; and protection of documents through the development of national and regional archives.

Part of the International Cooperation, Macro-Policy and Economic Coordination Department, CARP is headed by a full-time co-ordinator. A steering committee of seven senior government officers provides policy guidelines. The World Bank is an important and valued partner of the project.

FOREWORD

Asmara is far from a conventional urban environment, and, as mayor, I am the first to admit that many momentous challenges in managing the development of this remarkable city must be faced. Preserving, renovating and rehabilitating an internationally important urban centre, while aspiring to develop it so that it is equipped with twenty-first-century facilities, requires an enormous undertaking. Though Eritrea's tumultuous past has meant that it is deprived of vital experience and resources, there is a unique collective spirit and a stoic determination among Eritreans to progress.

It is with enormous pride and pleasure that, as a representative of the municipality and as a citizen of Asmara, I am able to witness the publication of this book that celebrates Eritrea's capital. Its true value lies far beyond the fact that it is a celebration of Asmara, however, since it is also crucial in highlighting the importance of respecting the wider significance and beauty of the city inherited by modern Eritreans, and of understanding better its remarkable development so that its future growth is founded on careful planning. Such responsibilities must be shouldered not only by many professionals and practitioners but also by all residents of Asmara, through their integral participation at grassroots level. This book therefore both appeals to Eritreans to value their precious capital, rising to the challenge of nurturing and involving themselves in its positive development, and also projects our heritage to the international community.

Eritreans are able to present to the world a heritage that is worthy of international acclaim and of which they should all be proud. This book therefore appeals to Eritreans to offer an unending commitment to future generations that this legacy is preserved, and to rise to the challenge of nurturing and involving themselves in the positive development of their capital, which will serve to make it one of the world's most atmospheric, interesting and, importantly, safe cities.

With an agenda based firmly on the needs of Eritreans, including the alleviation of poverty and the nurturing of a balanced and equitable society, we are seeking to achieve these aims. Through a tremendously constructive relationship with the Cultural Assets Rehabilitation Project we have been able to establish a 'historic perimeter', designed to secure the lasting preservation of Asmara's most valuable structures and public spaces, to plan the restoration or complete renovation of many of the city's most significant buildings, to upgrade city parks and other public areas, and, not least, to set about improving living standards for all our citizens.

Therefore I call upon individuals, communities and organizations, domestic and international, to collaborate in achieving these aims, and to ensure that it is not only Asmara's fascinating history that is recognized but also its bright future. For those who have witnessed Asmara's inimitable appeal only through the pages of this book, I extend my warmest greetings on behalf of all Eritreans and look forward to welcoming you to our home.

Semere Russom

Semere Russom
Governor of Zoba Maekel and
Mayor of Asmara

ASMARA
CITY MAP

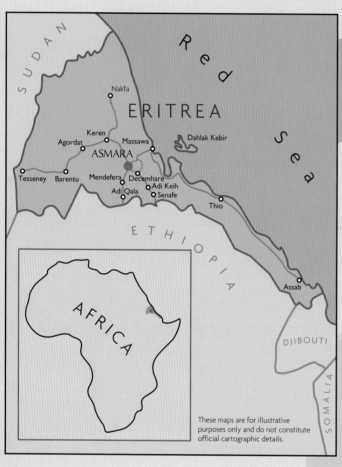

SUDAN

ERITREA

Red Sea

Nakfa

Keren
Agordat · Massawa
ASMARA · Dahlak Kebir

Tesseney · Barentu · Mendefera · Decemhare
Adi Qala · Adi Keih
Senafe

Thio

ETHIOPIA

Assab

DJIBOUTI

SOMALIA

AFRICA

These maps are for illustrative purposes only and do not constitute official cartographic details.

Key

	Major Road
	Minor Road
++++++++++	Former Railway (currently under reconstruction)
- - - - -	Historic Boundary
◼	Green Areas
◼	Rough Ground
✝	Church
☾	Mosque
✡	Synagogue

0 m   100 m   500 m
APPROXIMATE SCALE IN METRES

TO KEREN

IMBADERHO STREET

MAI BELA AVEN

ADI SHMAGLE STREET

HAWAKIL ST

ADULIS STREET

ARERIB STREET

MARYAM GMBI ST

BEILUL STREET

DENDEN

172-4 ST

HAWAKIL ST

QOHAYTO ST

172-5 ST

172 ST

172-2 ST

BEIRUT STREET

ALGIENA ST

DEBRESALA STREET

172-2 ST

DGSA 172-2 ST

172-4 ST

MEREB

189-8 ST

MEREB STREET

AGAMET STREET

189-6 ST

AENDALO STREET

KOKEN STREET

GOLIJ STREET

DGSA STREET

HIMBOL STREET

TEGADELTI ST

178-4 ST

MEREB STRE

189-1 ST

189-4 STREET

AR STREET

AR STREET

173 STREET

189-2 ST

AENDALO STREET

ABENEHE STREET

DBDB STREET

DBDB STREET

ABO STREET

AYLET

ADJUKUD STREET

ABO HAGAZ STREET

DEQ SHAHAY 187-8 ST

187-1 ST

BAQLA STREET

KUDO BERGENAST

745-4 ST

WARSAY STREET

ADJUKUD STREET

METETEN STREET

DERA STREET

Tiravolo

TO THE SOUTH

KSAD STREET

MAI MELAXE

HARAKA ST

ADI HADAS

ADI UKUD STREET

HIMBO STREET

TEGADELTI STREET

LABA STREET

FAH STREET

KUDO BERGENA ST

AORBABO STREET

KERVEBET STREET

746-2 ST

RUBA STREET

HARAKA STREET

HXEYLO

746-5 ST

746-9 ST

KUMAYLE STREET

745-7 ST

ABENEHE STREET

746-1 ST

TO THE AIRPORT

745-1 ST

BADA STREET

746-3 ST

RBDA STREET

EMBAHARA STREET

INTRODUCTION

ASMARA: AFRICA'S SECRET MODERNIST CITY

High in the mountains forming the northernmost reaches of Africa's mighty Rift Valley seems an unlikely location for an urban idyll. However, on a plateau at an altitude of well over two kilometres (more than a mile), high above the clouds, is Asmara, the capital of Eritrea and one of Africa's most remarkable cities. Built mostly during the later 1930s by Italian colonists during the period of Fascist rule, and effectively isolated by subsequent conflicts, this extraordinary conurbation contains perhaps one of the highest concentrations of Modern architecture in the world. After Eritrea won its struggle for independence in 1991, its 'hidden capital' was revealed: Asmara reflected an extraordinary age long gone but was still thriving in an African highland milieu – the fusion of European Modern architecture with African highland culture resulted in a sublime urban environment that has miraculously survived to the present day.

Asmara is, by any standard, not simply a most convivial city, well planned and executed; its physical character – its architecture and urban spaces – also reflects strongly a range of influences from political ideology through to artistic experimentation. Though little over a century old, the city of Asmara incorporates a wide range of architectural styles and curiosities. The form of many of its most prominent buildings belongs to Rationalism – a distinctly Italian interpretation of the international Modern Movement – while the city also includes fine examples of Novecento, Neo-classicism, neo-Baroque, monumentalism and Futurism, and several adroit references to vernacular styles.

Constructed almost entirely between 1936 and 1941, Asmara was effectively a blank canvas on which its Italian colonizers were able to design and build their own urban utopia in East Africa.

The era when Asmara was constructed was one of bold visions, heightened nationalism and charged design ideologies. Also, owing to Asmara's relative obscurity and distance from Europe, the architects and engineers who came to practise there could escape the constraints imposed on their activities in the more conservative European environment, making it an even more exceptional city. The purpose of this drive for rapid development was to establish a magnificent urban centre in the new Italian colony and to create a home from home for the thousands of Italians expected to migrate there. The orchestration of many architectural projects at this time provided the physical fabric that would confirm Asmara's status as the capital of independent Eritrea half a century later.

The Italian campaign in Africa did not last long, however, as the Allied forces liberated Eritrea from the Fascists in 1941. Sadly, this did not secure Eritrea's freedom, and it was not until 1993 that official independence would be assured. During these five decades Eritrea had to endure many years of hostilities that effectively isolated it from the rest of the world. The trauma that marks much of Eritrea's history offers little to laud, save for the immeasurable selflessness of Eritreans in the legitimate pursuit of freedom. However, this complete urban environment was in fact preserved as a result of these hostilities. This was not only fortuitous but also bizarrely ironic, since the destructive forces of war, so often the ravager of cities, and political instability protected Asmara from subsequent ill-planned urban development, leaving it almost exactly as its creators intended.

With independence firmly secured and attention now focused on the urgent issues of development in all areas of Eritrean society, Asmara, as the capital city, has a central role to play. This role is both clear and complex, regional and national, traditional and progressive, for Asmara will be the home not only of most political, economic and cultural institutions that will support future Eritrean society but also of a large part of its population and commercial activities. This almost disproportionate significance within the wider national context raises critical issues concerning the ways in which Asmara needs to develop. The city must be spared the mistakes that often arise from hasty or miscalculated design decisions relating to issues ranging from nation-building to urbanization. Although rightfully proud of their capital city, Eritreans must now confront and surmount these diverse problems. The vital development of Asmara and the preservation of its unique urban environment need not be contradictory aspirations but instead mutually supportive. Indeed, to frame these two issues as conflicting is to

misunderstand completely the process of urban regeneration. As the evolution of Asmara continues, the successful design of its early urban environment should be the very foundation for progress, rather than an impediment to it.

This book traces the path that has led to this stage and highlights the often remarkable legacies of those who have helped shape Asmara. Such legacies extend beyond pure bricks and mortar to encapsulate human experience: Asmara's inimitable character has helped define a people as much as they have defined it. The success of this reciprocal relationship can be measured in the city's renown as one of the safest and most attractive urban environments in Africa or indeed the world. This book aims to capture some of Asmara's unique journey through history and the experiences of those who have travelled it, for the benefit of those unaware, perhaps, that such a journey has even occurred.

It is appropriate and necessary at this point to underline the objectives of this book and of the many committed individuals who have contributed to its conception. Like many towns and cities, Asmara requires fundamental development, framed in the context of needing to preserve a unique and internationally renowned heritage. Such a task would be considered demanding for the world's wealthiest countries or leading urban centres, but the transformation of Asmara, capital of one of the world's poorest countries, into a modern city will be even more difficult. There is a definite urgency in extolling Asmara's beauty before it is threatened irredeemably, to ensure that an agenda of preserving its historic architecture is maintained along with the nurturing of vital urban development and the raising of living standards for its inhabitants. Those who have contributed to this book and to the wider aims of the Cultural Assets Rehabilitation Project of Eritrea ask readers to take account of the manifold obstacles confronting such an important project, and to view the results with an open mind. If one aim alone might be achieved through this publication, it would be that, by granting Asmara the recognition it rightfully deserves as one of the world's architecturally magnificent cities, broader development in Eritrea may be encouraged.

ERITREAN ROOTS

Eritrea is a country little known or understood internationally, despite its relatively recent emergence into a world characterized by increasing globalization and cross-cultural awareness. It constitutes a small but strategically significant corner of the African continent, with more than one thousand kilometres (over six hundred miles) of Red Sea coastline. Situated on the Horn of Africa, at the crossroads of Africa, Europe and the Middle East, Eritrea is characterized by an intriguing diversity – culturally, climatically, environmentally and historically.

THE PEOPLE AND GEOGRAPHY OF ERITREA

Eritrea's small size belies a long and complex history dominated by an almost continuous struggle for control of its territory. These struggles have cost countless lives and caused unmitigated suffering to the peoples of this region, though they have also left behind an astonishingly rich mix of cultural influences, making Eritrea unique in the African continent. The territory that today comprises Eritrea has borne witness to the rise and fall of some of the world's greatest empires, has been for centuries a centre of international trade and has experienced exploitation by foreigners of its land and people, as well as that of the continent of which it forms part.

Nine different ethnic groups constitute the 3.5 million people living in Eritrea. The population is divided almost equally between Christians and Muslims, with a small percentage of Animists. It is therefore impossible to provide an all-encompassing definition of an Eritrean, though many creditable adjectives have been used to describe the people in the past. L.F. Cogliati, a visitor to Eritrea at the end of the nineteenth century, described the men as "slim" and "elegant, with regular features", while the women were "rather beautiful", but it was the children that were most colourfully described. They were called "little devils" by the Italians, and once described as "children with eyes of fire, slim figures, agile like gazelles and ... something diabolically attractive about them".[1]

Three regions with distinctive climates and topography divide Eritrea, which has borders with Sudan, Ethiopia and Djibouti. The temperate central portion, where Asmara lies, is elevated on the highland plateau that stretches from central Ethiopia in the south to Sudan in the north. The highland plateau is situated between two desert regions: the eastern lowlands, running parallel to Eritrea's coastline, on the Red Sea, and the western lowlands, which occupy the vast area extending to Eritrea's western border with Sudan, far beyond which lies the mightiest of all deserts, the Sahara.

Eritrea was officially declared a colonial state by the Italians on 1 January 1890, following the consolidation of their earlier gains in the south of the country, including the port of Assab, and later conquests in Massawa and other areas further inland. Before this date the territory within the present-day boundaries of Eritrea was a stamping-ground for various local rulers in their quests to gain control of all or parts of the region. According to the modern definition of national borders, Eritrea did not constitute a distinct 'state'. Its boundaries, like those of so many colonized countries, are a construct of colonial ambitions rather than of indigenous autonomy. It was to take a further century of colonial domination before the latter was realized.

For the purposes of this book it will be sufficient to outline only briefly the key developments that shaped the region in which Eritrea is now an autonomous political entity, as well as to

The archaeological remains at Qohaito

identify the roots of numerous cultural influences found in the region today, through which traditional customs have been established. The terms 'Eritrean', 'Ethiopian' or 'Abyssinian' are used in this book only in retrospect, since the peoples or locations described by such terms are often difficult to identify precisely through history. Any reference to 'Eritrea' before 1890 is done so only for simplicity and is not intended to include other areas of the region or their peoples, since this part of Africa was subject to mass migration and integration of peoples, and did not have any strict tribal, imperial or national borders.

HISTORY OF ERITREA FROM THE EARLIEST TIMES TO THE SIXTEENTH CENTURY

The name Eritrea derives from the Greek word *erythrean*, meaning 'red'. One of the earliest-known references to Eritrea is in Fragment 67 of Aeschylus: "There the sacred waters of the Erythrean Sea break upon a bright red strand, and at no great distance from the Ocean lies a copper-tinted lake – the lake that is the jewel of Ethiopia – where the all-pervading Sun returns again and again to plunge his immortal form, and finds solace for his weary round in gentle ripples that are but a warm caress".[2]

Archaeological evidence suggests that the plains and highlands of Eritrea were first inhabited as long ago as the seventh and eighth millennia BC. There were periods of significant immigration by peoples from southern Arabia throughout the first millennium BC. Throughout this period many trading routes that were to prove vital for the development and survival of the later Axumite Empire were established. Some of the most important of the numerous urban centres to prosper at this time were the ancient trading city of Qohaito high on the Eritrean plateau

A Turkish mausoleum in
the eastern lowlands

The port of Massawa in the
nineteenth century

(see page 19); the ancient seaport of Adulis, used by the Greeks and Egyptians; and the trading post of Metera, between the coast and the ancient city of Axum. The surviving archaeological remains of these ancient cities testify to the scale and complexity of early societies in this region and the urban centres they established.

The Axumite Empire flourished in the northern regions of present-day Ethiopia and southern Eritrea from the fourth to the sixth century AD and left many legacies in the region. These include the adoption of the ancient language of Ge'ez, from which the current Eritrean language of Tigrinya is derived; the official introduction and adoption of Christianity, with the assistance of Syrian missionaries; the consolidation of the region's supremacy as a trading route; and the formulation of a distinct architectural style, which still exists in various guises and is examined in detail later in this book. The Axumite Empire began to decline from the seventh century AD, following the continued rise of Islam in Arabia and parts of Africa. From the period of Axumite rule through to the early sixteenth century, control of the Eritrean region, especially the lowlands, was held by numerous different tribal rulers.

The Kingdom of Medri Bahri ('land of the sea'), with its trading, religious, cultural and administrative centre at Debarwa, just south of Asmara, emerged around the fifteenth century. It comprised the former highland provinces of Hamasien, Seraye and Ackele Guzay, and controlled the route to the maritime province of Semhar. The ruler of the kingdom was known by the title Bahr Negash.[3] Owing to its strategic importance, highland Eritrea was often a battleground for local rulers and such foreign invaders as the Turks, Egyptians, Tigrayans, Amharas and Portuguese.

One of the most legendary and powerful Bahr Negash was Yishak, who defended his territory valiantly from many foreign invaders, in particular the Turks. However, the people of Medri Bahri were often obliged to form a military alliance with the Turks in order to oust Tigrayan and Amhara invaders. The seventeenth-century Portuguese traveller Almeida clearly described this problem: "Usually all along that route there are large bands of robbers, which is what nearly all the inhabitants of the neighbouring places are ... they accord very little obedience to the Emperor and are hardly subjects more than in name ... they are rarely subject to the viceroys."[4] In 1578 the Amharas defeated the combined forces of Yishak and the Turks, and with the death of Yishak the power and influence of Medri Bahri gradually weakened. In the first half of the eighteenth century, power shifted from Debarwa to the feudal warlords of the Tseazega family. A rival ruling dynasty had also risen in neighbouring Hazega. These two powerful clans had firm control of highland Eritrea until the nineteenth century.

THE TURKS, ABYSSINIANS AND EGYPTIANS, AND THE ARRIVAL OF THE ITALIANS

The Ottoman Empire was a major player in the continuous power struggle for control of the region. The Turks had occupied the Eritrean coast in 1557 and later established control of significant areas of the territory. Although they were the predominant occupiers, there were numerous invasions by the Portuguese and by Tigrayan and Amhara rulers of highland Ethiopia in the sixteenth century. Turkish occupation was responsible for the introduction to Eritrea of further cultural influences, which are still visible in forts, mausolea (opposite, left) and the ancient heritage of the port city of Massawa (opposite, right). The Turkish presence in Eritrea lasted a further three centuries and was centred on Massawa, while the Eritrean highlands remained under the control of the local feudal warlords.

The most prominent and powerful ruler in the highlands during the nineteenth century was Ras Wolde-Michael Solomon (right) of the Hazega clan. He had a formidable and well-organized army and, according to local tradition, together with the Tigrayans challenged Egyptian territorial gains in Eritrea at the battles of Gundet (November 1875) and Gurae (March 1876). Egypt's presence in the region had steadily increased throughout the nineteenth century, and by 1865 it had control of the coastal areas of Eritrea.

Emperor Yohannes of Tigray and his right-hand commander, Ras Alula, objected to the growing military power and influence of Ras Wolde-Michael Solomon. In 1878 Yohannes sent Ras Bayru, one of his commanders, to oust Ras Wolde-Michael and take control of the Eritrean highlands. However, the latter inflicted a crushing defeat on the Tigrayan commander in a battle in

Asmara. Emperor Yohannes tried to negotiate with the "rebel Ras" through his mediator, Ras Alula, pledging to solve the differences between them peacefully. Ras Wolde-Michael was deceived; in September 1879 he was captured and sent to Tigray to languish in Adua prison. A power vacuum emerged in the Eritrean highlands, which the Tigrayans were quick to exploit.

In 1882 the Sudanese Mahdists forced the Egyptians out of the Sudan, and Egyptian control of the western and eastern lowlands weakened. In the eastern lowlands around the infamous Denkalia region – the hottest place on earth – power had always lain with clan chiefs of the Afar tribal group. During the sixteenth century the Denkalia lowlands had been under the direct control of the Sultanates of Aussa and Rehaita. The relations of the Afar people with the neighbouring people of Tigray were that of raid and counter-raid. The Tigrayans ravaged the now vulnerable highlands and lowlands. The frequent raids in the western lowland areas of Gash-Barka created havoc and decimated the local Kunama communities. The people of Eritrea's western lowlands, who had suffered terribly under this state of anarchy, were quick to seek protection from the next rulers of the region – the Italians.

The Italians were the last European nation to join "the scramble for Africa". Their first foothold was in Eritrea's southern port of Assab, near the border with Djibouti, where the French had already established a presence. In November 1869 the monk Giuseppe Sapeto, who had earlier set up a mission in Eritrea's northernmost city of Keren, negotiated the purchase of eighteen square kilometres (seven square miles) of land on behalf of the Rubattino Shipping Company from the local chiefs. Following a series of local insurgencies that had resulted in a withdrawal by the Italians, further land was purchased from the Sultan of

Rehaita in 1879 and 1880, extending Italy's presence ninety kilometres (fifty-six miles) along the Eritrean coastline and up to ten kilometres (six miles) inland. By 1882 the Italian government had purchased the land belonging to the Rubattino Shipping Company and proceeded to administer Assab directly. In 1885, however, the issue of the control of the port of Massawa, in which the Italians were involved, was to prove a defining event in Eritrean history. Competing interests between the British, the Egyptians and Emperor Yohannes facilitated the occupation of Massawa by the Italians. The British, who then occupied Egypt, were indifferent to the fate of the port, though they did regard the Italians as the lesser of two evils compared with the French. So, on 5 February 1885, the Italians were handed control of Massawa and consolidated their footing on the Eritrean coastline.

THE FORMATION OF THE ITALIAN COLONY

The Italians had ready allies in those threatened by the Mahdists in the west and in other local chiefs holding grievances against Ras Alula, now Emperor Yohannes's representative in Hamasien. The emperor was angry when he heard that the British had allowed the Italians to settle in Massawa and ordered Ras Alula to attack those who sided with the Italians. By 1886 the Italians had started to move inland and posed a direct threat to Ras Alula's rule. In 1887 he routed an Italian expeditionary force at Dogali, forcing the Italians to retreat. Incensed by their presence, Yohannes refused to consent to Italian requests to delineate the Ethiopian border some way inland from Massawa, assuming, rightly as it turned out, that any concession of land would only be followed by further demands. However, by 1888 Italian reinforcements had arrived in Massawa; together with the Mahdists in the west and the dissenting Ethiopian general

Menelik, who was already plotting with the Italians, they posed a serious threat to Yohannes's authority.

Emperor Yohannes, forced to make a move, attacked the Mahdists but was killed in the Battle of Matama in March 1889. This left yet another power vacuum in the Abyssinian hierarchy, leading inevitably to a contest for the title of emperor between Menelik, supported by the Italians, and Ras Mangasha, the official successor. Menelik emerged victorious, and the Italians reaped the dividends of their earlier diplomatic efforts. In May 1889 Emperor Menelik signed the Treaty of Uccialli with the Italians, which delineated an official border between Eritrea and Ethiopia. Changes of government in Italy and thus of policy towards its colony, together with numerous power struggles in the ranks of the Abyssinian princes, led to a series of renegotiations of the treaty that considerably complicated jurisdiction of the region.

The result of these new negotiations was Italy's official declaration on 1 January 1890, by a royal decree of Umberto I, of the state of Eritrea. The recognized boundaries did not, however, reflect certain realities, since the Italians had occupied some areas well inside Tigray, thereby souring relations with their former ally Menelik. By 1895 the Italians had effectively invaded northern Ethiopia, contravening the Treaty of Uccialli; this invasion led to one of the most important events in the history of African and European relations, the direct consequences of which would extend as far as the Second World War: the Battle of Adua, on 1 March 1896.

At the Battle of Adua Menelik inflicted a terrible blow on the Italians that would result in an enduring dent in their national

The methods used by the Italians
for surveying as they moved inland
from Massawa

pride and leave over 4000 Italian soldiers dead. The Italian defeat was the first ever of a European army by an African force. It took forty years to avenge, until Mussolini invaded Ethiopia in 1935, but in the meantime it led to Italy redefining its role and conduct in the region. After Adua the legitimacy and purpose of Italy's presence in Africa was questioned within the government in Rome, and anticolonialists argued for a complete withdrawal from Africa. Appeasement of the Eritrean community by the colonial administration became essential, since any uprising would no doubt have encouraged collaboration between Eritreans and Ethiopians and thus perhaps compromised entirely Italy's aims in Africa.

The first capital of Eritrea was the port of Massawa. From 1885 there remained some doubt among the Italians as to the political, economic and military sense in invading the highlands, then under Abyssinian control. To invite further conflict by advancing inland, which in the minds of many Italians at home was both senseless and worthless, remained a contentious issue. Illustrating this uncertainty, A. Bizzoni stated at the time: "Politically, militarily and even logistically, the distance between Massawa and Asmara is greater than the distance between Italy and Massawa".[5] However, in 1889, after a series of advances to take control of the highland plateau, Asmara was captured. In 1900 the capital of the Italian colony was moved officially from Massawa to Asmara, marking the centralization of power in the Eritrean highlands that altered permanently the social, political and economic fabric of the region and its development.

The plateau on which Asmara is located provides a perfect environment for settled communities: its relatively rich soil, reasonable level of rainfall and flat land suitable for tillage have enabled it to support a large population. Abundant forests once carpeted the Plain of Asmara, sustaining a wide range of flora and fauna and affording plenty of adequate shelter. The temperate climate also ensured pleasant living conditions – particularly agreeable to Europeans compared with the lowland desert areas of Eritrea – and a reliable supply of water. A travelogue written by an Italian woman in Asmara shortly after its establishment as the capital describes the Plain of Asmara being "whipped by Aeolus [the god of winds], visited each day by Jupiter Pluvius [the god of rain] from June to September, and caressed with such sweetness in the other months by Phoebus [the god of sun]".[6]

The origins of the magnificent capital city situated on the Plain of Asmara stretch back many thousands of years. Only six to ten kilometres (four to six miles) from Asmara's central business district are the suburbs of Sembel, Kushet and Mai Hutsa, where significant archaeological remains dating back to between 800 and 400 BC were recently discovered. These represent some of the earliest-known settled agro-pastoral communities in the highlands of the Horn of Africa. Advanced communities of farmers and artisans seem to have lived here, raising cattle, producing pottery, and engaging in trade and commerce.

Closer to the present city centre are the sites of four small settlements – the origins of Asmara itself. These settlements – Geza Asmeaa, Geza Guretom, Geza Shilele and Geza Serensir[7] – date back to the first millennium AD, when the region attracted slave traders from the coastal lowlands. Women and children were captured and sent into slavery across the Red Sea, a grim practice that continued for centuries and remains one of the most tragic aspects of African history. Oral tradition holds that the initiative to solve this problem came from the women of the four settlements. They met to discuss the increasingly critical issue of their security, and resolved to ask the men to address the problem by uniting under a common leadership. Failure to do so would result in the women refusing to cook.

Understandably, the men agreed, and the settlements united. The elders also adopted an elaborate security system at night, known as *leiti deretom*, that involved guards from each settlement manning observation posts at strategic points in the settlements, from where they were able to warn of any incursions.

The common name of the four settlements became Arbate Asmara,[8] which means 'the four united'. This area formed by these settlements is now situated to the north-east of the city, although before the Italians arrived it was located around the present Orthodox cathedral. Following the adoption of Christianity after the fourth century AD the Arbate Asmara community built an Orthodox church with a tablet in ancient Ge'ez that reads: "This is the Church ('Tabot') of the unified settlements of Arbate Asmara and the surrounding area." Four additional churches – of St George, St Kirkos, St Michael and St Gabriel – were later built on the site of the four settlements.

Little is known about the development of Asmara following the foundation of Arbate Asmara, but in 1866 it became the general headquarters of the most important indigenous ruler of the central highlands, Bahr Negash Gurade Zeray. The selection of Asmara as a base for the Bahr Negash suggests that it was

A late nineteenth-century
photograph of Ras Alula's fort, on
the site of present-day Asmara
(below)

Ras Alula's *agdo*, or dwelling, within
the fort to the south of the present
city centre (bottom)

considered superior to other traditional centres such as Debarwa.
In 1875 the Egyptians, who had occupied the coastal zone in
1865, raided Asmara, causing the population to flee. By 1885,
with the Italians occupying the coast and port of Massawa and
Ras Alula, appointed by Emperor Yohannes, controlling the
highlands, Asmara faced further upheaval. Ras Alula had a tiny
fort, consisting of several small huts overlooking the Plain of
Asmara, built on a small hill close to the present centre of the
city (left).

EMBRYONIC ASMARA, 1889–1922

General Antonio Baldissera,
with Fort Baldissera (also
known as Fort Biet Mekae)
in the background

Following the Italian occupation of the northern city of Keren on
2 June 1889, a force commanded by General Antonio Baldissera
(above), assisted by Ras Alula's bitter rival Balambras Kafel, arrived
in Asmara on 3 August 1889 and occupied the surrounding plain.
This event marked the beginning of Italy's presence in the

highlands, which was reinforced just over a decade later when
the capital of the colony was moved from Massawa to Asmara,
though much of the state administration had already been
relocated to the highlands by that time. At the beginning
of the Italian occupation Asmara's population consisted of
approximately 5000 Eritreans and 300 Europeans.[9]

EARLY ITALIAN COLONIAL POLICY

A full understanding of the development of Asmara requires
an appreciation of the wider context of its origins and the
objectives of its Italian colonizers. Despite the relative ease with
which Baldissera eventually conquered the Eritrean highlands,
there remained for some time a perception among Italians that
their presence on the plateau was far from secure and that their
personal safety was threatened, a phenomenon that in relation
to the colonies of other European countries has been termed
the "black peril". It is important to emphasize the perception as
opposed to the reality, as "violent crimes by Eritreans against
Italians were almost non-existent".[10] In the early years of their
campaign in Eritrea, fearing rebellion from the local population,
the Italians – like most colonizers in Africa – adopted a policy
of 'divide and rule' towards the local chiefs, burnt local villages,
and espoused brutal repression.[11] This caused widespread
resistance and opposition among Eritrean tribal groups in the
rural highlands and lowlands. Zemat Wed Ikud in Barka, Abubakar
Ahmed and Mohammed Nuri of the Saho, Abera Haylu of the
Hazega, and Degiat Abera were among the many tribal leaders who
fought Italian oppression. The Italians, in response, established
an infamous prison on the island of Nakura, off the Eritrean
coast. In 1899, 107 of the 119 Eritrean inmates, including the local
heroes Ali Osman Buri, Degiat Mahray and Blatta Gilay, managed
to escape to Ethiopia, where they continued their fight against

The tribal leader Bahta Hagos, who led an uprising against the Italians in 1894

colonial subjugation. The most famous uprising had occurred in December 1894, instigated by the native chief Bahta Hagos (above). These events, and losses at the Battle of Adua, magnified the Italians' insecurity. As a result, they were forced, paradoxically, to adopt a more moderate stance so as not to ignite local antagonism. From a military, economic or social point of view they could not afford antipathy from native Eritreans. It could have flared easily into widespread dissent and encouraged collaboration with other aggrieved peoples, including those in Ethiopia, resulting in very serious danger to Italian control of the region.[12]

During the late nineteenth century Italy was experiencing considerable unemployment, high population growth and urban migration, and economic instability. The prime minister, Francesco Crispi, and Leopoldo Franchetti, an "outstanding expert on Italian rural problems",[13] believed that Eritrea could provide a solution to some of these problems. Eritrea's usefulness in the eyes of the Italian government at that time was as a self-sufficient agricultural settlement, absorbing Italian labour and peasant farmers. To facilitate this role under an early colonial policy initiated by Franchetti extensive seizures of land were ordered, resulting in the expropriation of more than 50% of the cultivable land in the Eritrean highlands.[14] Such action inevitably raised widespread antagonism from the local population. Already suffering from famine and epidemics of diseases such as cholera, they were now made landless. In addition, the fabric of Eritrean society was ruptured, since the social organization of indigenous communities was directly connected to the ownership of land and to the complicated land-tenure system. However, the Bahta Hagos uprising, and losses at the Battle of Adua, made such policies unworkable. Again, the Italians were forced to adopt a more judicious

approach, this time in relation to agricultural policy, which effectively undermined completely the *raison d'être* for establishing a colony. This more cautious policy aimed to separate native landowners from their land by other means, such as the offer of jobs in the new market economy, which also helped to expand the labour market. By 1910 expropriation of land in the highlands was effectively halted, and agricultural policy focused on intensive farming in the western lowlands.

The situation facing the Italians in Eritrea at the end of the nineteenth century and in the early twentieth was certainly precarious. As Italy had failed in 1896 to achieve its objective of conquering much of the Horn of Africa, its presence in Africa received much criticism domestically, and demands for a complete withdrawal persisted. Some of the original aspirations for the colony, including the large-scale settlement of Italian farmers on Eritrean land, proved unattainable or simply unrealistic. These problems, compounded by the colony's unexpectedly limited natural resources and the severely restricted colonial budget, meant that doubts about the incentives for pursuing colonization grew stronger. The colony remained a financial liability to the Treasury in Rome throughout much of its existence. It seems that the decision to remain in Africa was based on Italy's earlier commitments: "Blood and money has been scattered there in abundance."[15]

When the colony had been formally established, it was important to define the rules under which it would operate. Despite the more measured approach adopted by the colonial administration in dealing with Eritreans, the underlying principle of the racial superiority of Europeans remained. It underpinned all the decisions that affected the way the colony developed, from urban planning through commerce and industry to social

The first dwellings around Campo
Cintato, with Fort Biet Mekae in
the distance

policy. Governor Ferdinando Martini commented on the
marriage between a Swedish missionary and an Eritrean in 1901:
"It is absolutely necessary for the government to reaffirm in
an open manner the superiority of the white race over the
black. ... The prohibition of marital union ought to constitute
an insurmountable barrier necessary for the protection and
maintenance of the prestige of our race. But the Swedish Mission
has demonstrated its lack of sentiment of such prestige."[16]
Successive colonial administrations, differing considerably in
their approach yet bound by lack of resources, found it very
difficult to enforce laws against interracial marriage, and it
caused many practical and ideological problems because so
many interracial relationships resulted in births. Over 25,000
mixed-race babies were born in Eritrea during the period of
Italian rule. The issue of interracial marriage, which was contrary
to Fascist ideology, was confronted brutally by Mussolini in 1938,
when he enacted strict racial laws, forcing the break-up of
families along ethnic lines.

The development of an urban centre in the early years of Italian
rule, besides providing the necessary framework to house the
new administration both physically and symbolically, occurred in
conjunction with the drive to establish Eritrea as an agricultural
settlement. However, as Italy's agricultural and economic policies
in Eritrea changed, the role of Asmara slowly shifted. By the mid-
1930s it had clearly become a springboard for Italy to achieve its
long-term objective – the conquest of Ethiopia.

CAMPO CINTATO AND OTHER EARLY ITALIAN
SETTLEMENTS

For many years after the arrival of the Italians, Asmara remained
a relatively small town, despite its political and military
importance in the region. As the seat of the Governor of Eritrea,
it was the primary representation of Rome's presence in Africa
until the invasion of Libya in 1911. The first three decades of
Italian occupation in Eritrea provided the foundation on which

Rows of *agdos* for the *askari* and high officials (left and below left), some of which can still be seen in Asmara (below right)

the subsequent immense development of Asmara would take place. The years 1896 to 1922 saw the design and initial execution of various urban plans addressing such major infrastructure as the supply of water and electricity, the provision of sewage disposal and the layout of an embryonic road network. They also proposed housing development and reflected the implementation of policies on segregation. While these plans addressed the need to establish a settlement for the Italians firmly in the new colony, they also indicate significant local influences, which in turn reveal the fragile foundations of the early settlement and its dependency on the indigenous population.

The Italian settlement began with General Baldissera's fortification, built on an area of relatively high ground in the centre of the Plain of Asmara, which he named Campo Cintato (opposite). It became the administrative centre of the early settlement of Asmara and the site of the Eritrean government over a century later. In 1889 this military camp housed the

quarters of the commander and visiting officials, post and telegraph offices, an infirmary, a canteen and kitchen, and stores. As the camp evolved, more dwellings were built beyond its perimeter walls, as well as a school established by the town's padre, Don Luigi Bonomi, for Italian children, sons of local chiefs and even orphans from the cholera epidemics. The offices and residence of the Governor of Eritrea were also built near those of the fort commander. One early account of the buildings in this area describes an "elegant little palace of a dark red shade with green shutters, a tin roof which had been decorated in an oriental style and where, to say the least, there was a love of economical cooking".[17]

Life in and around Campo Cintato was fairly simple: it is evident that the principal dwellings around the fort shared a vegetable garden, chickens and flower gardens. Next to the camp were regimented rows of *agdos* (above) for the Eritrean soldiers serving in the Italian army, the *askari*.[18] Interestingly, the *askari*

Nakfa Avenue, aligned directly with
Fort Biet Mekae in the distance

A map of 1895 of early Italian
settlements in Asmara; note the
course of the caravan route
running from east to west

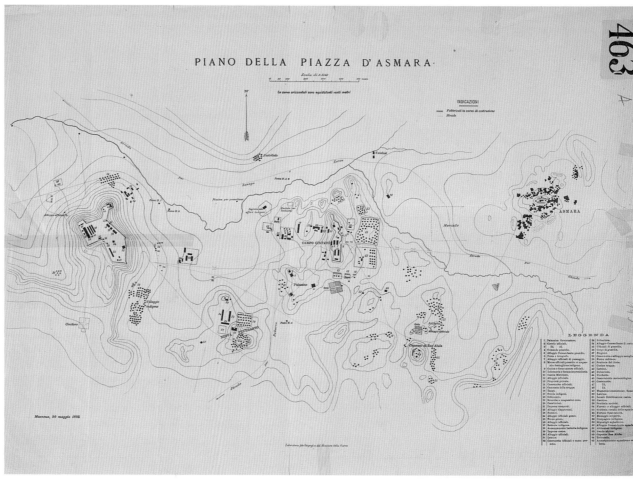

comprised Christians, Muslims and "foreigners" who appeared to put aside religious dogma and lived happily together.[19] Herein perhaps lies one of the roots of Asmara's much-admired congenial atmosphere and religious tolerance today, an idea that is further supported by the often-noted tranquility of the native villages despite the considerable density of their population. The uncharacteristic closeness of these dwellings to the Italian buildings indicates the level of trust that the colonial administration had in the *askari* from early on. This relationship lasted throughout the Italian occupation, and was possibly the most significant one between the Italians and the Eritreans. In 1926 Luigi Federzoni, the Minister of the Colonies, described the Eritrean regiments as being "the most solid, effective and safe pillar of our military might in all our African colonies".[20] Cogliati also spoke of the *askari*'s "battle spirit", which made them "truly very good soldiers".

Recognizing Campo Cintato's poor strategic position, General Baldissera ordered the occupation of the highest ground overlooking the Plain of Asmara, the site of the village of Biet Mekae and also of the city's present-day western border where the Ministry of Information is located. The construction of a fort there necessitated the displacement of the village and its inhabitants from the hilltop. To avoid conflict, the Italians paid the villagers compensation and had the village relocated, placing it under the protection of Italian cannons. Still anticipating retaliation from other native forces, including those of Ras Alula, Baldissera ordered the building of an impenetrable stone wall around the fort. With this means of defence Baldissera's fort had absolute command over the Plain of Asmara, and no enemy ever breached it. Named Fort Baldissera by the Italians, it remained known among the Eritreans as Fort Biet Mekae.

Between Campo Cintato and Fort Biet Mekae a small settlement named Nuova Peveragno was established shortly after 1890, with stables for mules and for horses of the cavalry, dormitories, accounts offices, a riding school and stores. Several such minor settlements appeared all over the Plain of Asmara. They included a Greek kiln, vegetable gardens, a hospital (on the slopes of Fort Biet Mekae), offices, law courts and numerous private buildings. In 1894 a third fort was constructed to defend the eastern flank of Asmara and to safeguard the main supply route from the coast and Massawa. Named Fortino Vigano, it was situated to the south of the road from Massawa and to the east of the settlements, an area known as "the gates of the devil". Renato Paoli, a visitor to Asmara in 1908, condemned the fort as "one of the many colonial blunders committed at those times", since it had insufficient positions from which to fire weapons and was "useless for defence", compounded by the fact that it had been disarmed.[21]

DEVELOPMENT TO THE WEST AND EAST OF CAMPO CINTATO

The town plan of Asmara remained centred on the relationship between the settlement around Campo Cintato and the single caravan route (opposite), later the road, that led from Massawa and the villages on the eastern escarpment, such as Nefasit and Ghinda, to the towns of Keren in the north and Adi Ugri in the south. On reaching the Plain of Asmara the route from the coast continued in a westerly direction, towards Fort Baldissera. The only point at which this straight east–west course is broken is where the road meets the hill on which Campo Cintato sits, which forces it to reroute to the south. The road therefore follows a predominantly straight course from east to west, but with a small 'dogleg' in the centre. The line of this road was

pivotal to the manner in which Asmara developed. It is evident
that the subsequent development of civic buildings, as befitting
the type of city that the Italians intended to create, occurred
along this road, to the east and west of the hill on which Campo
Cintato stood. On the western slopes the colonial administration
rapidly erected the buildings required to house the machinery of
government, while on the eastern side private and other public
buildings were also soon constructed.

To the west of Campo Cintato and north of the road, the new
administrative buildings consisted of a police barracks, finance
offices, soldiers' dormitories and officials' quarters. On the other
side of the road were the grounds of the Governor's Palace
(top left and above). This area was the centre of the colonial
administration, which operated with considerable independence
from the central government in Rome. The appointment of the
first civilian Governor of Eritrea, Ferdinando Martini, in 1897
marked the transition from a military to a civil administration.
His term of office lasted until 1907, when Giuseppe Salvago Raggi
replaced him. Between them Martini and Raggi, whose tenure
ended in 1915, were responsible for authorizing much of Asmara's
early development, which would support its later growth.

The grounds of the Governor's Palace contained the residences
and offices of the highest-ranking officials in colonial Eritrea.
Two identical *palazzine* and two other buildings arranged in
a triangle formed the nucleus of Eritrea's embryonic civil
administration. One of the *palazzine* was the governor's
residence, while the other housed the office of the military
commander. The two smaller buildings contained offices
and clubs. Father Bonomi also had a house in these grounds,
connected to which was a "microscopic" church.[22] Although
there appears to be no evidence of the church or the priest's
house today, the two existing *palazzine* are the oldest colonial
buildings in Asmara. By far the most significant development
in this area was the building of the new Governor's Palace,
commissioned by Martini and completed in 1905, between the
old residence and the smaller office buildings. This magnificent
Neo-classical structure was the centrepiece of Asmara's colonial
architecture to date. (For a more detailed account of the
grounds, see pages 88–92.)

The various commercial and public buildings constructed to the
east of Campo Cintato around this time included banks, the
central post office, shops and hotels. These early buildings sat
on either side of the east–west road that by now had become
the major avenue through Asmara and was named Corso del
Re ('street of the king'). It linked the new central Piazza Roma
(top right), protected by nearby Campo Cintato, with the east of
the city, where it joined the ring road and the road to Massawa.
A series of tombs once stood between this piazza and the
mosque square. Nearly all the original colonial buildings in this
area east of Campo Cintato still exist, the most notable of which
are the former tribunal with its distinctive portico, now the
central post office administration building (see page 97); the
former Albergo Italia, built in 1899 and one of the oldest

Early European single-storey dwellings in the Eritrean highlands

View from the former fort of Ras Alula, showing early Italian dwellings and the original Catholic church

buildings in Asmara (see page 96); the imposing building on the east side of Piazza Roma, once owned by the Eritrean Salt Company and presently occupied by the Commercial Bank of Eritrea (see page 99); and the idiosyncratic, Venetian-style Bank of Eritrea building (see page 100).

THE GRID SYSTEM, DEVELOPMENT IN THE SOUTH OF ASMARA, AND MAI BELA

As the centre of Asmara grew in the first years of the twentieth century, the grid system employed in the early development of the town was designed to accommodate subsequent expansion. The deliberate employment of a grid system might have been intended also as a symbol of 'civilized' order, transcending the organic disorder of indigenous settlements and underlining Italy's 'superiority' over its colonial subjects. However, the undulating topography of the Plain of Asmara did not in fact suit a rigid system, as an early traveller to Asmara noted:

> I say the 'flat ground' of the city, but instead it is anything else but flat. Light undulations, little hills, mounds, bumps, dips and little valleys in the ground bring a truly picturesque variety to the buildings and to the streets, which therefore never appear similar to one another. They offer suitable areas and remarkable positions in which to make public buildings prominent. In short, it is a ground so made that it would be the torment of a builder from Turin, the horror of an engineer from America, but would be dreamt of by an architect who is truly artistic, a lover of the picturesque, and an enemy of uniformity.[23]

The slightly irregular patterns of building in the early development of Asmara are evident today in the network of narrow streets and

one- and two-storey buildings around the old Piazza Roma and former Campo Cintato. The single-storey buildings in this area and the small villas to the south, in the Quartiere dei Villini, testify also to the modest nature of the development of Asmara in its early years (above, top). These relatively simple, unostentatious structures would not be the subject of academic critique, but they do represent perhaps the best example of a modern Italian 'vernacular' architecture adapted to the Eritrean highlands. Bearing no monumental attributes or symbolism and little decorative moulding, such buildings resemble the *architettura minore* of Italy and are, as Bertram Goodhue wrote of similar buildings elsewhere, "of minor importance, but in consequence, of greater direct, practical value".[24] Such buildings in the European quarter of Asmara were subject to strict regulations that determined their height, size and proximity to neighbouring buildings, and stipulated that all walls be plastered and painted.

Between the early commercial area and the river the Catholic mission was established. Situated on the banks of the Mai Bela River and forming the eastern edge of the European quarter, this became the religious heart of the Italian community. The mission began modestly, with the first, small Catholic church built in 1895 (above), but it grew swiftly to include a nursery, school, printing press, convent, library, priest's residence and

The exterior and interior
of a *hidmo*

An *agdo* in the Eritrean highlands

even a theatre. The present cathedral, finished in 1923, replaced the smaller church (see page 110).

The Mai Bela River, running south-east to north-west through the city, provides the most striking obstacle to attempts at establishing a grid system in Asmara's early street plan. According to legend, on the banks of this river the Queen of Sheba gave birth to her son, Menelik, by King Solomon; from him descended the bloodline of the Solomonic princes, the last of whom was Haile Selassie. The course of the river was normally dry, but it became a veritable torrent during the rainy season, when the native population used to wash their clothes there by beating them on animal hides with the soapy seeds of the phytolacca tree. Although early town plans accommodated the course of the river, it was filled in between 1936 and 1937 and converted into a major traffic route. At the very start of Italian occupation the Mai Bela had provided a natural boundary, albeit largely symbolic, between the emerging European quarter in the west of the city and the 'mixed' and native areas further east. This boundary ceased to exist as numerous bridges were built across the river. Corso del Re traversed the city over the largest bridge, made of stone, linking the elements of the city along one primary axis; this route was later superseded by the larger Viale Mussolini to the south.

INDIGENOUS ARCHITECTURE AND ITS INFLUENCE

Although the first manifestations of Italian Asmara included the areas west of the Mai Bela, it is important to acknowledge the existence of indigenous villages occupying the Plain of Asmara, which predate the arrival of the Italians by over 1000 years. Before Baldissera's fortifications, the only buildings on the Plain of Asmara were traditional dwellings for the local

population and nobility, and an Orthodox church serving the village of Arbate Asmara (see pages 134–35). The location of this church, then in the centre of the village, is particularly important since it is the site on which the Orthodox cathedral stands today. Aesthetic references to this continuing tradition appear in the architecture of the present Orthodox cathedral, built in 1938 (see pages 134–35). Traditional dwellings and their methods of construction are certainly noteworthy. Two types of dwelling are broadly found in the Eritrean highlands: the *hidmo* (above, left and centre) and the *agdo* (above right). (The term *tukul* is more commonly used, albeit incorrectly, to describe the *agdo*.) Furthermore, the 'monkey-head' construction technique, which is indigenous to this region, was also common around Asmara.

The *hidmo* is a substantial structure, fabricated from wood, stone and soil and found only in the Eritrean highlands. As each one uses wood from up to one hundred trees, the construction of these buildings is no longer feasible owing to the lack of trees in the highlands. A *hidmo* is generally rectangular in plan, with at least two partitioned areas inside and a flat roof. Entry is through the main doorway at the front of the building, with one or two other doors at the rear. An extended roof at the front acting as a veranda, known as a *gebela*, covers the entrance and provides shelter for livestock at night. Inside the *hidmo* are areas designated for preparation of food, for meetings and for sleeping. Earthenware food silos often act as partitions between these areas. In larger *hidmo*s owned by the wealthy or noble, a reception hall is used for meetings and feasts. The average *hidmo*, which might last more than half a century, incorporates twelve tree trunks supporting the weight of a roof constructed from layers of branches bonded with soil, while its stone walls are often close to a metre (three feet) thick.

An *aderash*, or two-storey building

The 'monkey-head' technique in wood, combined with such contemporary materials as concrete and mortar

The *agdo* is a more modest dwelling found in most areas of Eritrea. Circular in plan and measuring approximately three metres (nine feet) in diameter, the *agdo* has walls formed of only stone and soil, with a conical grass roof. There is only one entrance, and the interior is often divided into two areas across its widest point. Cooking is usually undertaken outside. The *tukul*, identical in form to the *agdo*, has walls constructed of straw and sticks, rather than stone and soil. Such impermanent buildings were probably designed for livestock or storage rather than as human dwellings. Two-storey forms of the *agdo*, known as *aderash*, are very rare, but where they do exist they denote a religious building or the house of a high-ranking individual (above left). The building techniques of both *hidmo* and *aderash* were also used in traditional churches.

A unique vernacular construction technique called the "monkey-head" predates both the *hidmo* and the *agdo*. It takes its name from the use of protruding, rounded-off wooden cross-members (dowels) to bind together horizontal layers of wood between layers of stone in a wall (above right). These protruding dowels look like the tops of monkeys' heads. This technique preceded the use of lime mortar, which was introduced to Eritrea from Yemen in the mid-seventeenth century. Used extensively during the Axumite period, the 'monkey-head' technique was designed to bind the wall and provide support, while making use of available resources. Evidence of its use existed in Asmara when the Italians arrived and can still be seen, albeit superficially, in some buildings, as well as in the pre-Axumite ruins at Qohaito.

The fact that these three construction techniques were widely employed on the Plain of Asmara when the Italians arrived is important for understanding both why the Italians adopted

certain references to vernacular Eritrean architecture in some of their buildings, and the way in which the location of these structures, as well as that of the early Italian settlements, determined the eventual layout of Asmara. The market where the two communities came to trade with one another, together with the settlement and Orthodox church of Arbate Asmara, are significant reference points adopted in subsequent urban plans. In the position of these early structures lay the foundation of Italy's policy of segregation in Asmara.

URBAN PLANNING IN ASMARA IN THE EARLY TWENTIETH CENTURY

The transition from a military to a civilian administration (with the first civilian governor, Ferdinando Martini, taking over from the military governor Oreste Baratieri in 1897) assisted Asmara's early development. A team of civil engineers replaced the

The west end of what is now Harnet Avenue, before it became a major thoroughfare in the late 1930s

military engineers who had laid the early foundations. The constant financial restrictions imposed on Eritrea by Rome, which hindered further development of the colony in this period, would remain a contentious issue between the central and the colonial administrations.

In 1908 the Italian government approved the first significant town plan for Asmara, following the scrapping of a plan proposed in 1902. The earlier plan had focused primarily on improving public hygiene and concentrated only on the Italian community around Campo Cintato, placing less emphasis on other public works and ignoring the indigenous quarters. This disregard by the administration for the indigenous areas of Asmara remained a common thread in urban planning throughout the colonial period and was particularly apparent towards the end of Italian rule; it has remained one of the worst legacies of colonial maladministration in Asmara. The

military hospital on the eastern slopes of Fort Baldissera was expanded as part of this plan in response to the increasing outbreaks of certain diseases among both Italian and native populations. Such outbreaks fuelled the myth among Italians that native Eritreans were the source of disease, which in turn served to reinforce the Italian policy of racial segregation in urban planning. The hospital itself was divided into two, with the native wards kept some distance from the Italian wards for fear of cross-infection.

In the 1908 plan, segregation took the form of four distinct urban quarters. The first, accommodating Europeans only, comprised the areas to the west of the Catholic mission (including the city centre) and to the south (including the European residential area). The second, a 'mixed' quarter for Europeans, other foreigners (such as Jews, Greeks and Arab traders) and Eritreans, centred on the market. The third was the quarter for the indigenous population, around the Orthodox church and to the north of the city. The fourth was an outlying area reserved primarily for industry. Unlike the layout of many other colonial cities, which reflect the implementation of grand master plans with little regard for pre-existing settlements, the division of Asmara into these four districts was determined by the location of such elements as Campo Cintato and the Governor's Palace, the Mai Bela River, and the native market and village of Arbate Asmara with its Orthodox church. In effect, Asmara's development was founded on a curious amalgamation of pre-existing social and physical realities overlaid by a racially predisposed socio-economic policy of development.

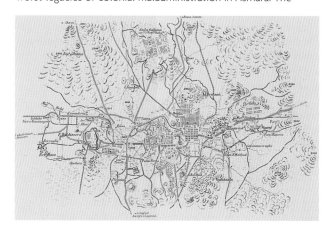

A map of Asmara in 1906; note the grid system in the European areas and the rows of *agdo* for *askari* north of the market

The first Italian Colonial Congress, held in Asmara in September–October 1905, gave Governor Martini an opportunity to outline

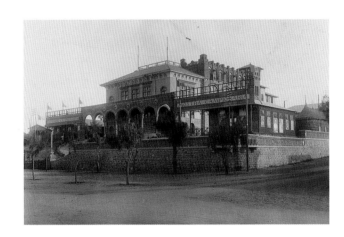

the progress made by Eritrea's civil administration in its first years. The congress underlined the need to improve living conditions in the colony, and to set in motion a scheme of road building and appropriate land distribution that would facilitate further migration from Italy without causing undue dissent among the landed locals. The establishment of essential regional infrastructure, such as wells, aqueducts and telegraph networks, and the construction of markets, caravan stations, post and telegraph offices, health centres, schools and churches marked the early years of Asmara's development.[25]

A third plan, drawn up in 1913 in Asmara's new Civil Engineering Office by the city's chief engineer, Odoardo Cavagnari (1868–1920), altered many aspects of the designs of 1902 and 1908, but the earlier attempts at racial segregation, and the four previously established zones, remained (see pages 38–41). Its primary aim, however, was to provide for the inevitable expansion of Asmara, particularly in the European zone, with a street layout that stretched far beyond the existing city limits in every direction. In the following year further plans were ratified for the detailed development of various zones. The purpose of these urban plans was to provide a pleasant and functional urban environment, reminiscent of home, for the Italians, and also to contain and control the native population, which consistently far outnumbered the Italian community. There was no substantial provision in these plans for most of the indigenous population, who were forced to live to the north of new industrial areas in often unplanned settlements in the north-east of the city. Those who had property in the city centre were often forced to sell their land and move out.[26] Far from being the ideas of individuals, the proposals for segregation in these urban plans – which appeared in those of all other colonial cities before

Asmara – were the outcome of extensively reviewed and discussed issues within official government forums and architectural circles, reflecting the institutionalization of discrimination at that time.

Within the city centre the proposed street layout illustrated a shift in importance from the original Corso del Re to a new thoroughfare to the south, which soon after was named Viale Mussolini. Another major east–west thoroughfare to the north of the city but parallel to both Corso del Re and Viale Mussolini was proposed. The entire city centre, including Corso del Re and the market, was thus effectively sandwiched between the two new roads. The only significant road bisecting them would be that of Mai Bela, which after being converted from a river in 1937 would run in the direction of the proposed suburb of Gheza Banda in the south-east to the Keren road in the north-west.

With the future Viale Mussolini earmarked as the primary thoroughfare, the construction of the city's then largest buildings began about 1920. The first was the Asmara Theatre, designed in 1919 and completed in 1920 (see above and pages 105–08). Assuming a commanding position at the west end of Viale Mussolini as it rises towards Campo Cintato, this eclectic building was one of the last works of Odoardo Cavagnari. It exhibits a distinctive exterior of brick, stone and plaster, and a characteristic facade sporting a portico composed of seven arches overlooking a sweeping double staircase to the gardens and street below. The completion of the theatre signalled an expansion of the social life of Asmara and provided an important venue for the nascent arts scene in Eritrea. A second building to rise on the north side of this fledgeling thoroughfare was the

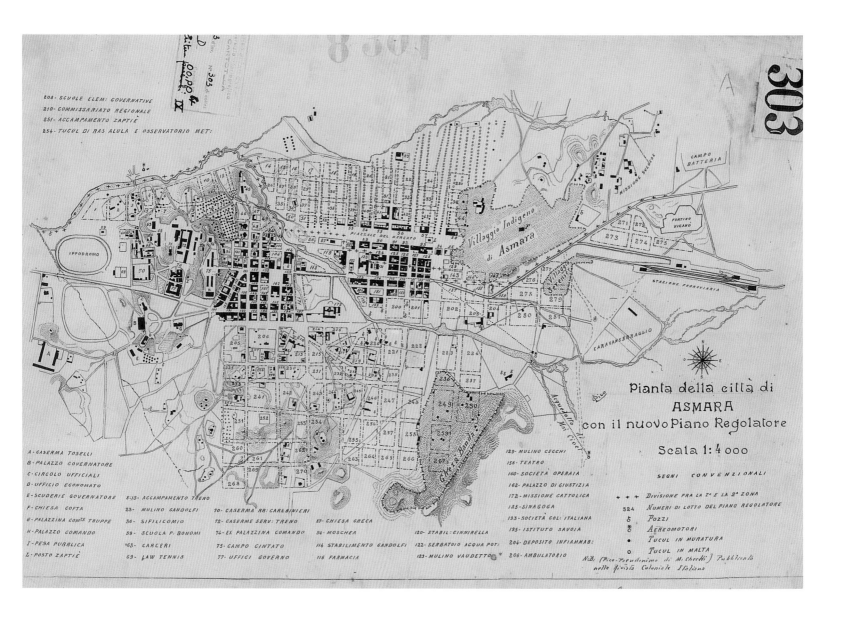

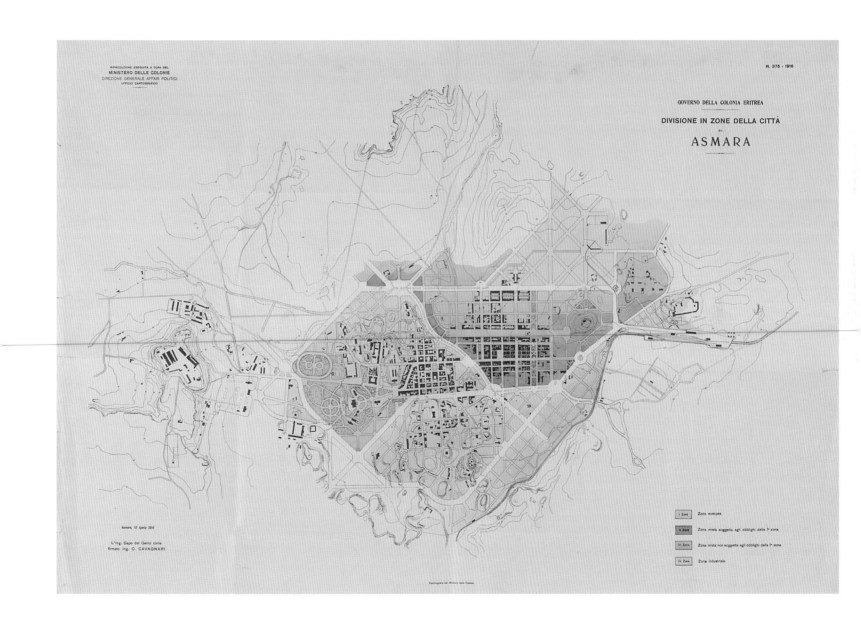

Cavagnari's plan of 1916, which was a refinement of his plan of 1913, illustrating the strict zoning of the city

Cavagnari's plan for Asmara,
drawn up in 1913

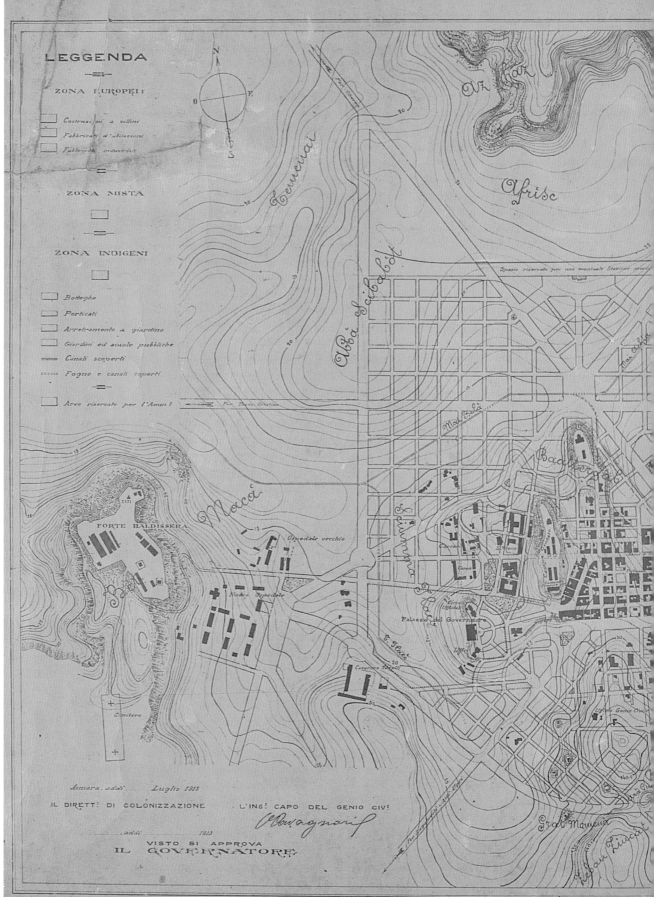

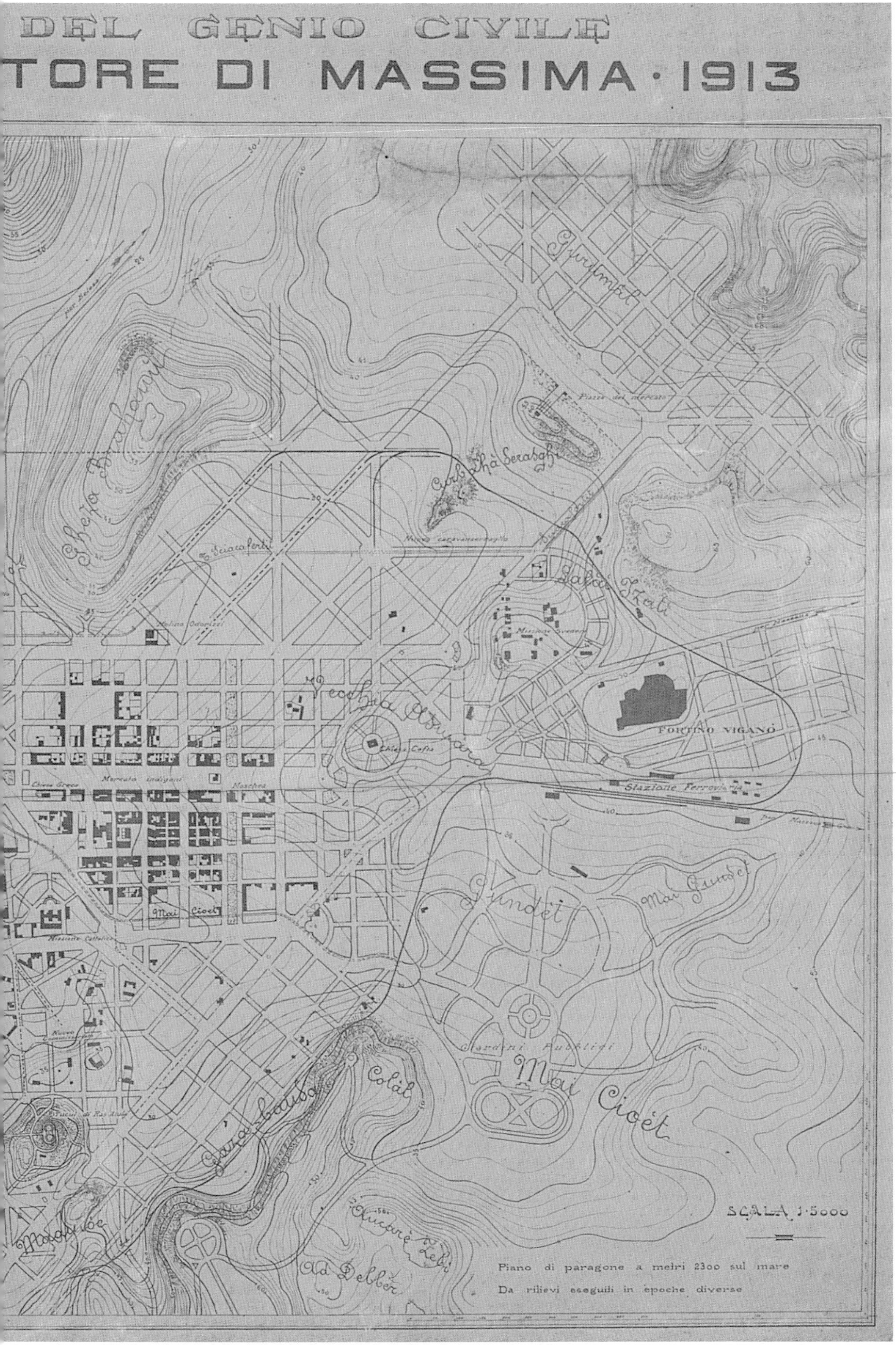

Piazza del mercato

Caravanserraglio Serabghi

Nuovo caravanserraglio

Sciaraferti

Mining Sveven

Lago Itali

Molino Odorizzi

Vecchia Asmara

FORTINO VIGANÒ

Chiesa Copta

Chiesa Greca

Mercato indigeni

Moschea

Stazione Ferroviaria

Mai Cioet

Missione Cattolica

Sundet

Mai Sundet

Nuovo

Giardini Pubblici

Mai Cioét

Colái

Gasa Daiba

Rascal di Ras Alula

Aucorè Zeli

Ad Debber

SCALA 1:5000

Piano di paragone a metri 2300 sul mare

Da rilievi eseguiti in epoche diverse

41

The Catholic church of Kidane Meheret, built for the Eritrean Catholic community in the 1960s

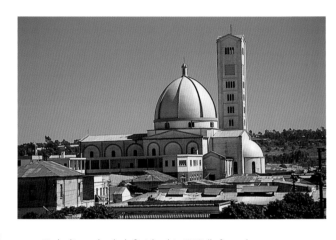

The Catholic cathedral, completed in 1923

new Catholic cathedral, finished in 1923 (left, and see pages 110–11). This building replaced a much smaller church that had stood since 1895, originally established by the Italian Capuchin Order and the Sisters of St Anna (see page 110). Designed by the architect Oreste Scanavini and built in brown brick in the Lombard style, the new cathedral, with its commanding location and towering campanile, dominated the city.

In 1920, to the south of the city centre and at the foot of the hill on which Ras Alula once had his fort, another important addition to Asmara's skyline and Eritrea's new political institutions was taking shape. This was the Commissariato dell'Hamasien, the headquarters for the municipal and regional administration (see page 109). Built in a medieval style, similar to that used in elements of the theatre and the later Casa del Fascio, this symmetrical, two-storey construction overlooking what are now manicured public gardens was one of Eritrea's principal state buildings. It was built in an ostensibly residential quarter, and the choice of its location, given the political significance of the building, remains curious.

OTHER RELIGIOUS BUILDINGS, AND THE DEVELOPMENT OF THE RAILWAY

The city of Asmara was well endowed with religious buildings from soon after its foundation. The Eritrean Catholic community had a church built in a vernacular 'monkey-head' style northwest of the market in 1922. This was later destroyed and replaced by a much larger church in the 1960s (above). As in the region's many monasteries, the interiors of Orthodox churches were often bedecked with paintings in the Orthodox style (opposite, top left), similar to the Byzantine, and were used for the secure storage

Traditional Orthodox
monastery paintings

Traditional religious artefacts
inside a monastery

View of Asmara from the roof
of the old mosque, in the 1910s

of scriptures, manuscripts and other sacred artefacts (top right).
The original Orthodox church, of Arbate Asmara, in the form of a
hidmo, was a very simple structure resembling more a "cave than
a temple".[27] It was replaced in 1920 by a modern structure built
by an Italian engineer, E. Gallo, the decoration of which emulated
the layered "monkey-head" construction employed in its
predecessor (see pages 134–35). The new church was a rectangular
building behind two square towers, and was itself replaced by
the Orthodox cathedral in almost exactly the same style in 1938.
At the entrance to the courtyard in front of the church stood
another building, Degghi Selam, designed in 1917 by Odoardo
Cavagnari, in which the decoration of the cross-beams that
supported the roof also imitated the 'monkey-head' technique.

Both the towers of the church by Gallo and the building by
Cavagnari had conical concrete roofs imitating the grass roof of
the *agdo* (see pages 134–37). These were two of the first structures
to illustrate the willingness of some Italians to incorporate
allusions to the aesthetics and materials of vernacular styles.
Until the Italian invasion, architects and engineers knew little

about such styles and so did not fully acknowledge them. This
attitude contrasted with the endorsement and imitation of
the Moorish styles of North Africa and the Middle East in
the construction of modern buildings in such cities as Tripoli,
Mogadishu and even Massawa. It is unclear whether this earlier
failure to refer to Abyssinian highland styles was a result of
the prevailing ignorance among Italians of these vernacular
methods of building compared with their knowledge of Islamic
architecture, or a reflection of the greater respect paid to the
latter than to the former, which were perceived as 'primitive'.

The construction of the Catholic mission's first church in 1895
marked the start of a spate of new religious buildings on the
Plain of Asmara. A mosque was built about 1906, owing to the
growing number of Eritrean Muslims living there. The area
around the mosque has remained the Muslim quarter, and a new,
larger mosque was constructed on the same site in 1938 (see
pages 130–33). The Swedish Protestant mission, located in the
north-east of the city, constructed a church at the end of the
nineteenth century and had a large compound of buildings,

The synagogue, built in 1905

The Greek Orthodox church

The railway sheds in Asmara

including four schools that provided education to orphans. The small Protestant community still worships in this area of Asmara, but a larger, modern church has replaced the original. The existing Greek Orthodox church, with a miniature bell-tower, was constructed on the south side of the market early in the twentieth century (opposite, right). Finally, a small synagogue, built in 1905 in a Classical Greek style, remains a testament to the Jewish community of over five hundred people that once thrived in Eritrea (opposite, left). They are said to have migrated first from Turkey and later from Italy and Aden.

Another important development, towards the end of 1911, was the extension of the railway from Massawa to Asmara (right). Work on Eritrea's magnificent railway network started in 1887, when the Italians were moving inland from their foothold in Massawa. By 1904 the railway had reached Ghinda (altitude 888 metres/2880 feet) and by 1910 Nefasit (altitude 1672 metres/ 5430 feet). Between Nefasit and Asmara, with an average gradient of 1:30, labourers had to construct over twenty tunnels and sixty-five bridges and viaducts. Designed initially to assist the trade and export of goods to the Middle East from western Eritrea and Sudan, the railway was intended to link up with the Sudanese network. Progress was delayed significantly owing to the First World War, and the railway reached only slightly beyond the western lowland town of Agordat (altitude 606 metres/ 1970 feet) by 1928; construction never resumed. Roads were also improved: following the First World War Asmara's unsealed streets were in some cases metalled or paved.

By 1922, after over thirty years of slow, incremental development, Asmara was emerging as a small city. It would still be more than a decade before it became a stylish metropolis, but, with a new

government and a new leader in Mussolini at home in Italy, the period from 1922 onwards would change the course of Italian history and that of its colonies. The events of the 1920s and 1930s would contribute to unimaginable destruction in all corners of the globe, but Asmara would escape this and remain largely isolated for a further fifty years.

View of Asmara, showing the four distinct zones of the city: the native quarter in the north, with its high density of buildings and irregular layout; the diagonal blocks of the industrial zone; the medium-density mixed zone around the market; and the salubrious European quarter to the south

EMERGENT ASMARA, 1922–35

A view from Gheza Banda of Asmara in the 1930s

A Fascist propaganda poster

Despite the relatively favourable outcome for Italy of the First World War (and the personal achievements of the soldier and journalist Benito Mussolini), the country was to face increasingly severe upheavals during the post-war years. In a period of weak government and political and economic turmoil, the rise to power of Mussolini and his Fascist Party, advocating disciplined government and economic prosperity through free-market mechanisms, was almost inevitable. With Mussolini's popularity spreading rapidly from his northern Italian strongholds, his threat of a march on Rome, and the extreme impotence and inefficiency of Italy's state administration, King Victor Emmanuel III had little option but to invite Mussolini and the Fascists to take over the government, which he did on 29 October 1922.

ITALY, ETHIOPIA AND THE BRITISH

It soon became clear that Eritrea's strategic importance as an Italian outpost in north-east Africa would increase. This signalled an unprecedented period of growth and development for Asmara (above right), as Mussolini prepared to realize his vision of "Africa Orientale Italiana", an Italian empire in East Africa to match the grandeur, pomp and expansionist tradition of the Roman Empire long before. This scheme required the invasion of Ethiopia, in 1935, to avenge the defeat at the Battle of Adua forty years earlier and to impose in East Africa the Fascist state's "will to power and domination" through "territorial, military and mercantile expressions" as well as the "spiritual and moral".[28]

The goal of controlling Ethiopia would take longer than Mussolini expected. The reasons for this lay in the numerous and complex issues surrounding the Ethiopian question at this time. Under the leadership of Prince Ras Tafari (later as Emperor Haile Selassie)

Ethiopia applied for membership of the League of Nations on 30 July 1923. With their presence in Djibouti secure, the French supported the application in an attempt to curb British and Italian influence in East Africa. Despite various protests from other countries at Ethiopia's inclusion in the League, particularly over issues of lawlessness and the ongoing slave trade within the empire, its membership was ratified on 13 October 1923. Italy's publicly declared support of the ratification (notwithstanding its earlier disapproval) would haunt its government for many years to come. With Ethiopia a member of the League of Nations, it was impossible for Italy to annex the country without incurring the full wrath of other member states. Italian diplomats predicted a collapse of the unstable Ethiopian empire, which would allow Italy to extend its influence from its relatively small stronghold in Eritrea. This disintegration proved as illusory as the promised cessation of slave trading, and the Ethiopian issue would continue unresolved in the eyes of the Italians and within the League of Nations until 1935.

Richard Lamb's book *Mussolini and the British* highlights an interesting and crucially important postscript to this early chapter in Italian–Ethiopian relations, and illustrates the agreement between the British and the Italians regarding the extension of the influence of both nations in Ethiopia. The British had attempted for several years to seek approval from the Ethiopian government of a scheme to construct a barrage at Lake Tana, to benefit irrigation projects in Sudan and Egypt. The Italians knew of the scheme, since they had offered their co-operation back in 1919, but Britain had refused their support. The Italians were not acting entirely altruistically, since they were seeking British support for their own scheme to build a railway linking Eritrea with Italian Somaliland, which would

The former Fiat Tagliero service station

traverse Ethiopia. Such a project would have required the constant protection of Mussolini's army, since tribal uprisings in Ethiopia were common, and thus effectively would have allowed Mussolini to enter Ethiopia through the back door.

With relations between Britain and Italy warming by 1925, Sir Ronald Graham, the British ambassador to Rome, and Mussolini met to discuss the project. The Ethiopian government, again supported by France – whose monopoly of the Ethiopian railway system was at stake – appealed to the League of Nations, claiming that its sovereignty was being threatened. The League forbade any further interference in Ethiopia by the Italians. The matter was dropped until 1935, when Mussolini, with some justification, pointed out that "England only recently regarded Abyssinian independence as an absurdity. In 1925 Sir Ronald Graham and I signed an Agreement which practically cut Abyssinia to pieces." Lamb suggests: "Indisputably the Graham–Mussolini agreement of December 1925, coupled with the admission of Abyssinia to the League of Nations in 1923, were important factors in bringing about the Abyssinian War of 1935, which in turn contributed to the causes of the Second World War." These events would drag Eritrea unwillingly into the maelstrom of war along with Italy.

Futurist styling on a building on the former Mai Bela River, constructed in the late 1930s

NEW MOVEMENTS IN ART AND ARCHITECTURE: ART NOUVEAU, FUTURISM AND NOVECENTO

While these and many other world events that would impact directly on Eritrea's social, political and economic structures were taking place, much was also happening in international circles of art and design that would have an equally important effect on the physical environment of Eritrea, and in particular of Asmara. During the 1920s designers throughout the world

The Colonia Marina XXVIII Ottobre dormitories in Cattolica, Italy

attempted to break the shackles of traditional styles and approaches, which they considered were hindering the attainment of a contemporary, 'modern' reality. The twentieth century had started with the first modern design movement, Art Nouveau – 'Arte Nuova' or 'Stile Liberty' in Italy – which "burst into the [Italian] public's consciousness with the First International Exposition of Modern Decorative Art in 1902".[29] It advocated a radical move away from traditional forms, sourcing its styling instead from nature and amorphous organic structures. As calls for an original, distinctively Italian style grew louder, so criticism of the universality and superficiality of Arte Nuova became stronger. In 1914 the architect Marcello Piacentini declared: "The arid and tormented period of the *stile moderno*, the plebeian banality of *arte nuova* is over."[30]

For some, but by no means for all, hope of a modern revolution appeared in the emerging movement of Futurism. It celebrated the new machine age and its dynamism as the antithesis of all things traditional, which were deemed irrelevant and mundane. Launched as a fine-art movement in 1909 with Filippo Tommaso Marinetti's *Manifeste du futurisme* (published in Paris), Futurism enveloped architecture in 1914 when Antonio Sant'Elia published his *Manifesto dell'architettura futurista*. As in the case of the Rationalists, several years later, the Futurists' youthful exuberance and revolutionary zeal were among their trademarks. Some Futurist influences can be observed in Asmara's architecture. The most obvious example is the Fiat Tagliero service station, designed in 1938, which has enormous cantilevered concrete wings, like the shape of an aeroplane, a machine that the Futurists admired beyond all other (see page 49, top). Another, more obscure, example is the locomotive form of a building on Mai Bela, the sweeping shape of which, as it descends down Mai

Bela from Corso del Re, gives the structure an undeniable sense of motion (see page 49, centre). Similar in style are the Colonia Marina XXVIII Ottobre dormitories in Cattolica, Italy, designed by Clemente Busiri-Vici and built in 1932 (see page 49, bottom).

By 1921 it seemed that a truly Italian modern style had emerged in the guise of Novecento, of which the leading exponent was Giovanni Muzio. His Ca' Brutta ('ugly house'), built in 1922 in Milan, which became the centre for Novecento architecture, marked the first physical manifestation of a building style "which indisputably was the first sign of modern architectural taste".[31] It is very difficult to provide a definitive description of Novecento, owing to numerous different interpretations. Although Novecento architecture was deemed 'modern', it originated both as a contemporary adaptation of Classical styles, including references to vernacular architecture, and as "a modern analogue to the Neo-classical past".[32] Herein lies an implicit link between Novecento and other classicizing tendencies, as part of the 'return to order' throughout European architecture after the First World War.

Novecento used simplified Classical forms and ornamentation, modulated surface decoration and raised or sunken panelling to imitate traditional Italian architecture. The surface decoration characteristically employed on the facades of Novecento buildings – particularly low-cost, large-scale housing projects built on open, green urban spaces – was intended to refer to the 'cosy rusticity' of the past. This presents a paradox, as explained by R.A. Etlin: "The irony of the decorative Novecento style was that it was developed for buildings that were transforming Milan into a taller, more crowded, busier city. All it could offer for the loss of the city's bucolic pleasures were nostalgic signs evocative of the recent past."[33]

Terragni's Casa del Fascio,
Como, Italy

An imitation in Asmara of
Terragni's Novocomum building,
by the Italian architect Antonio
Vitaliti on Harnet Avenue

Terragni's Casa del Fascio,
Como, Italy

An imitation in Asmara of
Terragni's Novocomum building,
by the Italian architect Antonio
Vitaliti on Harnet Avenue

RATIONALISM AND FASCISM

By the late 1920s the Novecento style was facing competition from another modern movement in architecture and design, known as Rationalism. This new style was a distinctly Italian variation of the International Style or Modern Movement increasingly popular elsewhere in Europe, and a response to the theories of architecture expounded by Le Corbusier in his *Vers une architecture* (1923) and Walter Gropius in his *Internationale Architektur* (1925). Unlike Novecento, Rationalism claimed to be "particularly attentive to functional requirements and constructed with modern materials made into forms that evoked the spirit of a machine civilisation".[34]

Rationalism advocated the application of logical thought processes to create rational design solutions. The external appearance, the structural and tectonic integrity, and the careful understanding and employment of materials, light, colour and interior furniture should all contribute to explaining the functionality of the building.[35] Dismissing ornamentation as unnecessary, Rationalist architects focused only on the aesthetic result of the scientific and logical arrangement of the building components. As a theory intimately connected with the science of construction, the concept of rationalism therefore underpins all aspects of architectural practice. Entwined with this emphasis on logic and function was a genuine concern for social responsibility, expressed particularly in projects for low-cost housing and in the social aspects of urban planning, which had a strong influence on architecture in Eritrea, though not for several years. Rationalist architects also engaged in the design of furniture and other products, in which low cost would often be a primary consideration.

The origins of Italian Rationalism, like Novecento before it, are found in and around Milan, but the manner in which the two movements emerged was very different. In December 1926 a series of explosive articles advocating a new form of Italian architecture, written by a group of seven Milanese architects, calling themselves Gruppo 7 ('Group 7'), thrust Rationalism into the public realm. As Etlin points out, the name of the group continued the type of anonymous labelling used by earlier avant-garde art movements, such as "the Belgian painters who founded Les XX [The Twenty] in 1884 [and] the Berlin artists who in 1892 launched the Gruppe der Elf [The Group Eleven]".[36] One man whose work would come to exemplify Rationalism was Giuseppe Terragni, an architect from Como, near Milan. His work, like that of other Rationalist architects, was grounded in Modernist contextualism found also in Novecento. Some of Terragni's most influential works are in Como and include the Novocomum apartment building (1927–29; opposite), the War Memorial to the Soldiers of Como (1931–33) and, most important of all, the Casa del Fascio (Fascist Party Headquarters; 1932–36; above left). Interestingly, in 1944 in Eritrea an Italian architect named Antonio Vitaliti designed a building on Asmara's central thoroughfare, Harnet Avenue (above right), that almost replicates the form of the Novocomum. After the defeat of Italian Fascism such an explicit reference to one of Rationalism's foremost buildings might be deemed a moderately nostalgic architectural gesture.

Rationalism had begun with no firm political allegiances, but in 1931 the Second Italian Exhibition of Rational Architecture in Rome "argued for the official identification of Italian Rationalist architecture with Fascism".[37] A circular from the Movimento Italiano per l'Architettura Razionale (MIAR) clearly indicated this

Water supply and sewage disposal pipes being laid along Viale Mussolini in the 1930s

Construction of roads in the European quarter in the 1930s

intention by stating: "If the renewal of Italy is taking place in the political-economic-social field through the Fascist Revolution, little renewal is occurring in art and nothing in architecture. We Rationalist Architects, as Italians and as Fascists, cannot and must not permit the architecture which has only the decaying aspects, the cadaverous forms, to be passed off as Fascist architecture."[38] As part of the 1931 exhibition, a room known informally as the "panel of horrors" displayed photographs of ten buildings by eminent Italian architects that claimed to conform to Fascist ideology – a claim that the Rationalists refuted vehemently. Naturally, this incurred the wrath of the eminent architects and their supporters. Like the Futurists before them, the Rationalists felt duty bound to liberate themselves, their work and the Italian public from bourgeois traditionalism and the unacceptable "impotence" of older architects.[39]

Mussolini inaugurated the exhibition on 30 March 1931, but this act was not intended to signal the régime's allegiance to the

Rationalist movement. Fascism promoted artistic diversity, both modern and traditional styles, and chose not to adopt any particular stylistic imagery or language as its own, unlike the extremist political movements of Germany and Russia. "The entire point of Fascist cultural politics was to embrace all aspects of Italian intellectual and artistic life as vital signs of a full flowering of Italian creative and artistic genius under the aegis of Fascism. ... In all phases of intellectual, cultural, artistic, and social life, Fascism was like a voracious amoeba: it swallowed everything around it in order to proclaim that it was all a Fascist achievement."[40] Nevertheless some in Italy saw Fascism as the saviour of traditional forms of art, which had been so eroded by the advance of modern technology and the "atheist materialism" encouraging the redefinition of artistic practice, particularly in photography and film.[41]

DEVELOPMENT OF ASMARA IN THE 1920s AND EARLY 1930s

Despite its strategic importance, Asmara remained relatively small until the mid-1930s. From 1895 through to 1935, just before Italy's invasion of Ethiopia, Asmara's Italian population rarely exceeded 4000, with up to 100,000 indigenous Eritreans living in traditional dwellings around the city's perimeter. In the years immediately following the invasion, the Italian population in Asmara rose to well over 50,000. Throughout the 1920s and early 1930s the expansion of Asmara remained incremental. Work undertaken involved mainly the consolidation of some building projects and infrastructure, such as the construction of reservoirs, introduction of sewage disposal systems, and improvement of road and pavement surfaces (above, left and right).

Architectural styles remained largely eclectic, with no significant consensus or stylistic direction among colonial architects and engineers. This eclecticism is visible in most of Asmara's key buildings constructed before 1935, all of which display a blend of styles including elements of Classical, Lombard, Romanesque, Renaissance, medieval and even vernacular forms. Truly eclectic architecture embodies the belief that no one aesthetic should dominate to the detriment or exclusion of others. It involves not direct imitation but instead an organic reorganization of a wide variety of forms with reference to their original historical context.

Examples abound in Asmara of the usage of this stylistic language, though the most obvious is probably Cavagnari's Asmara Theatre, built before 1935, which references Romanesque and Renaissance architecture (see pages 105–08). Another example is the former Palazzo Minneci, next to the central post office, built after 1935, which has a Neo-classical ground floor of half-columns supporting a strongly Novecento upper facade (see pages 177–79).

Before 1935 the most significant addition to the now well-established Viale Mussolini was a building (now the Ministry of Education) constructed on the block east of the theatre (see pages 122–24) and designed in a similar style to its neighbour, with a plaster and brick exterior and arched portico. Built in 1928, it housed a club for government officials, which became the Casa del Fascio (Fascist Party Headquarters). Its elevated position overlooking the street was both symbolic and practical, representing the dominance of the Fascist Party and its status in the city. However, in the early 1940s the building's design was changed, in order to characterize better the spirit of the mature and hardened Fascist movement.

By the mid-1930s, as an Italian invasion of Ethiopia became increasingly probable, it was obvious that such a move would have a profound effect on Asmara. The city as it stood in the early 1930s was clearly inadequately equipped to cope with the developments planned for the rest of the decade. In anticipation of this dramatic expansion, a decree in 1933 ordered the enlargement of the European zone and an extensive programme to be conducted by the Office of Public Works that included the rearrangement and paving of the streets; provision of a widespread sewage disposal system that encompassed even the 'mixed' areas of the market; implementation of a telephone and radio network; expansion of the Queen Elena Hospital; and renewal of the electricity network. Development on an unprecedented scale was required to cope with the massive increase in population after 1935. The six years between 1935 and 1941 would prove a defining period in the growth of Asmara.

The Casa del Fascio, and part of the Asmara Theatre, during the construction of Viale Mussolini (now Harnet Avenue)

53

BURGEONING ASMARA, 1935–41

A poster encouraging Italian
agricultural workers to
migrate to Africa

The cable car linking Asmara
with the coast

Asmara in 1937 – the Cinema
Impero is under construction
in the background

A poster encouraging Italian agricultural workers to migrate to Africa

The cable car linking Asmara with the coast

Asmara in 1937 – the Cinema Impero is under construction in the background

On 3 October 1935 Mussolini embarked on fulfilling his vision of an Italian empire in the Horn of Africa by crossing the Ethiopian border and taking Adigrat and Adua, the latter the scene of Italy's defeat by the Ethiopian army under Menelik in 1896. By taking revenge on Ethiopia for almost forty years of national dishonour, Mussolini flouted the authority of the League of Nations and opened the floodgates of conflict that would lead almost inevitably to the Second World War. Germany looked on, while the victors of the First World War were divided and in disarray.

This chapter of Asmara's history is characterized by unprecedented growth and the transformation of a relatively provincial city into a highly sophisticated metropolis, the most modern city in the whole of Africa. Much of Asmara's development took place in a broader context of racial intolerance. It is important to note, however, that explicit, hard-line prejudice against non-Europeans only emerged towards the end of Fascist rule in Italy. Eritrea's

distance from and relative obscurity in relation to Rome ensured that often a distinctly diluted, and sometimes contradictory, form of Fascist dogma appeared in Asmara and elsewhere in Eritrea.

THE EXPANSION OF ASMARA AND CONDITIONS FOR NATIVE ERITREANS

The build-up of Italian troops on the borders of Ethiopia inside Eritrea and Italian Somaliland in 1935 had followed many months of preparation. Asmara became a major base for Italy's invasion of Ethiopia, as over 50,000 Italian civilians and soldiers arrived in the city to establish new lives in the new East African empire and help create the infrastructure to support its burgeoning population (above left). In Asmara more houses were being built, particularly in the European areas in the south of the city; the world's then longest cable car (above centre), at over seventy-five kilometres (forty-six miles), was constructed to transport goods from Massawa to Asmara; existing roads were asphalted and new ones laid down; the first civil aviation route between Rome and Asmara was established; and hundreds of Italian businesses set up offices or factories in the colony. The Italian population of Asmara peaked at around 70,000 by the end of the 1930s.[42] Such an influx of people in so short a time necessitated ambitious urban planning and building projects. The construction of almost the entire city between 1935 and 1941 left an indelible and fundamental impact on its later form and style (right, and opposite, right).

Many thousands of construction workers, labourers, artisans, craftsmen and painters arrived in Eritrea from Italy, easily finding work among the hundreds of building projects that were being carried out simultaneously. There was a high demand for Eritrean labour – cheaper than Italian – but the way in which the many thousands of Eritreans helped to build the environment that one day they would inherit is not well documented. Workers in the city (and elsewhere in Eritrea) dug trenches for water and sewage pipes, installed power lines and substations, painted buildings, prepared cement, quarried granite for the paving of streets and laid bricks. Life for a colonial subject living and working in Asmara was not easy. Labourers had to contend with the searing heat, the dry, dusty terrain and the vicious thorns of the acacia bush while constructing the seventy-five kilometres of cable-car line linking Asmara with the coast. Eritrean labourers received pay of half a *lira* a day with wheat flour for rations while at work. Compensation for injury was non-existent.

Those Eritrean men not in the labour force were probably risking their lives as *askari* for the Italians in Ethiopia, Somalia and Libya. The Italian army included an unusually high percentage of indigenous soldiers compared with most colonial armies, which probably had some bearing on the level of respect paid to Eritreans by their colonizers. Italy employed 60,000 *askari* during the war against Ethiopia in 1935.[43] However, many deserted to the Ethiopian side to fight against colonial oppression and Fascism; Haile Selassie once said: "[Many Eritreans] came over to us and joined our ranks. The part played by the Eritrean people in the Ethiopian resistance movement was extremely important." The Italian policy of recruiting *askari* had several purposes. As wage-earners they were able to support their families in times of drought, alleviating some of the burden on the colonial administration. (Nevertheless, wages for Eritreans, whether *askari* or other workers, remained very much lower than those received by Italians. *Askari* received 1.5 *lire* per day, later cut to 1 *lira*.)[44] The administration could also encourage greater loyalty from

Construction of buildings on Viale Mussolini; an image of Mussolini's face can be seen on the hoarding

The Viale Mussolini and Mai Bela roads being laid down

The 'native' quarter of Asmara

Cafiero's 1938 plan for the development of Asmara

Eritreans if they were direct employees. Finally, the Italians were able to allay fears at home of the potentially high numbers of Italian casualties in various conflicts if they could employ more *askari* in battle. The colonial army in Libya actually contained more Eritreans than it did Italians.[45]

Eritrean women provided most Italian families with manual labour in the home; some families had many maids to carry out the daily housework. They were required to be loyal and obedient; they worked long hours and sometimes received no pay, since a roof over their heads and food were considered sufficient recompense. Training was provided for Eritrean medical staff so that they could treat the indigenous population in Queen Elena Hospital. For women unable to find such 'respectable' jobs, there was always a high demand among Italian men, soldiers in particular, for Eritrean concubines and prostitutes.[46] The demand was fuelled by the enormous imbalance between the numbers of single Italian men and women. Statistics from 1913, published by Francesco De Angelis, showed that of the 1373 single Italians in Eritrea, only 73 were female.[47] Despite a law restricting it, prostitution became so widespread that the administration had to turn a blind eye.

Mussolini's imposition of racial law in 1938 had resounding and dire consequences for many in Asmara. The movement of Eritreans within and between areas with newly imposed boundaries in the city became tightly restricted, and they were excluded totally from some areas, especially at night. The city's relatively unhindered development before 1935 – despite the policy of segregating Italians and Eritreans – had in fact facilitated a greater degree of racial interaction and toleration than in many other colonial cities of this time. As discussed

above, the reasons for this are numerous and complex, but essentially Italy's weak economic and social position in Eritrea did not allow for the isolation of the European community deemed necessary or desirable elsewhere. Such interaction was not achieved through any altruism inherent in Italian colonialism *per se* but was, without doubt, a consequence of necessity rather than humanity.

URBAN PLANS OF THE LATE 1930s

Seeking to consolidate their position after the Ethiopian campaign, the Italian Fascists began to devote their attention to civilian matters, and an important set of initiatives in town planning and architecture for Italy's new colonies was set in motion. One such initiative, announced on 24 July 1937, was the competition for the master plan of Asmara that would expand on the earlier designs implemented by Cavagnari. The "Terms of Reference" for the competition stipulated the separation of ethnic groups, and the representation of the power of the Fascist state in the layout of the city and the style of its buildings. The author of the "Terms of Reference" was the architect Marcello Piacentini, who presumably had the blessing of Mussolini himself. Piacentini postulated that "all buildings should in the final analysis be expressions of a certain [*i.e.* Fascist] will". The stage was set for the creation of a Fascist master plan for Asmara.

Far from watchful eyes in Rome, the colonial governor in Asmara, Vincenzo De Feo (governor from April to December 1937), took matters into his own hands and established a commission to oversee the competition and nominate a winner. Numerous entries were submitted, including an entry entitled "Divina geometria" ("Divine geometry") by a visionary architect and

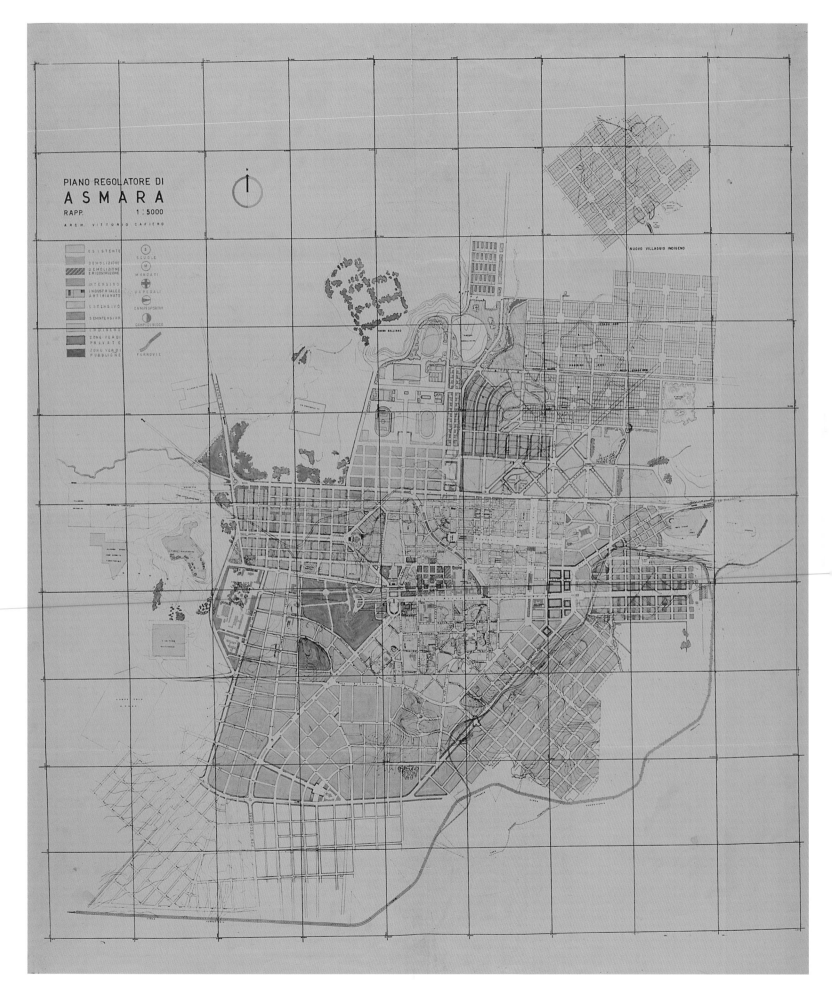

PIANO REGOLATORE DI
A S M A R A
RAPP. 1:5000
ARCH. VITTORIO CAFIERO

57

Corso del Re in the late 1930s,
looking west (right)

Viale Mussolini (far right)

engineer named Guido Ferrazza, who had worked in Libya before arriving in Eritrea and had considerable experience in other Italian colonies. However, the commission announced a project called "Sannita" as the winner, awarding the successful architect 10,000 *lire*. "Sannita", a rabidly racist master plan with a strictly defined ghetto for non-Italians, was in fact designed by De Feo himself, which caused immediate controversy. Architects who had taken part in the competition protested vehemently. The matter was referred to the government in Rome, which found the criticisms legitimate and rescinded the competition. De Feo was quickly replaced by a new governor, Giuseppe Daodiace, who had served in Tripoli.

Governor Daodiace brought with him Ferrazza, a sensitive man who abhorred the idea of creating a master plan designed to separate the Italians and Eritreans and was concerned about the living conditions of all the city's inhabitants. In this he seemed to have the support of the governor. Ferrazza was able to implement significant elements of his plans that can still be seen, albeit incompletely, around the market and mosque squares. Ferrazza and Daodiace were fortunate that control by the Central Council of Town Planning in Rome over the plans for Asmara became gradually less pronounced as Fascism faced greater challenges in Europe.

However, the architect Vittorio Cafiero was sent to Asmara in 1938 to provide a new plan for the city (see page 57). This was a difficult assignment, because Asmara had already developed quite extensively; certain patterns of urban growth had emerged that would be problematic, even impossible, to alter; and discontent among those involved in the competition debacle of the previous year still simmered. Cafiero was aware of these

problems, though the new racial laws imposed by Mussolini both provided a reason for and made it necessary to implement certain changes to make the city "tidy and functional". In carrying these out, Cafiero emphasized the zoning of the city to distinguish its varied functions. Certain practical considerations of balancing the requirements of commercial, industrial, residential and leisure areas needed attention, but central to the plan was the separation of the races.

To achieve this, Cafiero utilized the unique 'mixed' quarter as a buffer zone or 'diaphragm' between the strictly Italian district and the indigenous areas that had been pushed to the extreme north-east corner of the city. This 'diaphragm', around the bustling market areas, would ensure that "the only contact of the whites with natives will be with the highest category of them, the commercial and industrial one".[48] (The fact that the native tribunal was situated at the western end of the market square meant that local villagers had another reason to frequent this area.) The hill of Emba Galliano also provided a 'green' barrier between the native and European quarters. The density of population in the native quarter, as outlined in Cafiero's plan, is very much higher than in the Italian quarter, at 380 and 140 inhabitants per hectare (two and a half acres) respectively.[49] Such proposals illustrate Cafiero's aim of meeting the demands of the Fascist policy on race by depriving the native inhabitants of sufficient area for housing. Racist views were also espoused by Attilio Teruzzi, Vice-Secretary of the Colonies, who, while implementing policies to support his iniquitous beliefs, was still able to bemoan the "lack of initiative and poverty of the native, who still does not have the need of a nice, clean, solid and airy house, in a few words, a decent and hygienic house".

Futuristic designs of the late 1930s
for kiosks in Asmara

DEVELOPMENTS IN HOUSING AND INFRASTRUCTURE, AND AROUND VIALE MUSSOLINI

Living conditions in Asmara for native Eritreans were poor. The 'native' quarter of Asmara remained chronically neglected, in terms of its urban planning, architecture and provision of services, and therefore evolved quite differently from the rest of the city. No broad formal street plan or infrastructure existed to ensure adequate health care, communications, education or sanitary facilities for the indigenous population. There was, and remains, no running water in houses, streets were left unsurfaced (and remain so), and electricity was not installed; no adequate measures were ever established to ensure satisfactory and appropriate improvements in the future. These virtual shanty towns were subjected to much less stringent planning regulations than the European quarter and therefore supported dwellings built with mud and stone, and occasionally brick. These buildings were arranged haphazardly but were usually maintained impeccably by their owners. The legacy of this continuous neglect by successive colonial administrations remains to the present day in the form of Asmara's most deprived suburbs, ignored by subsequent administrations until Eritrea became independent owing to the controversial political and economic issues surrounding them. (The chapter on Future Asmara details this issue.)

For Italians, however, life was considerably more comfortable. By 1941 the European areas of Asmara afforded basic services for water supply, sewage disposal and health care. The broad paved streets — lined with flowers, shrubs and trees, lit by electric lamps, patrolled by police and with more traffic lights than

The centre of Asmara in the early
1930s, looking north-west

A view of Asmara in 1936,
looking west

The transformation of Mai Bela from a water course into a thoroughfare

An unexecuted design dating from 1937 for a hotel and shop complex along Mai Bela, which would have blocked the road

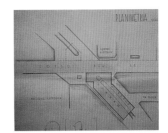

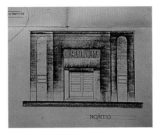

Design for a cinema for the indigenous population, near the market square

Rome[50] – were part of an almost surreal European landscape that also included ostentatious villas and lavish gardens. Early consolidation of the "delightful zone of the villas [Quartiere dei Villini] ... a zone which is rich in trees and flowers"[51] to the south of Viale Mussolini meant that additional housing for new arrivals in Eritrea had to be constructed in entirely new suburbs such as Gejeret and Gheza Banda, which had featured in earlier plans for the city. Cafiero's plan also anticipated the need to deal with the increasing problem of car ownership. By the late 1930s there were 50,000 cars in Asmara (an average of one per Italian inhabitant), for which the infrastructure was still woefully inadequate.[52] This problem severely affected the creation of a new urban street plan.

What emerged in the European areas of the city was a well-planned and well-executed urban environment that not only satisfied the immigrant Italians' persistent nostalgia for their motherland but was also equally suited to its African context. Light, dynamic and modern, the new buildings in these areas represented the spirit of progress and adventure that characterized the Italian colonial experience, and were far removed from those of the 'native' quarters. The preservation and co-existence of the European and indigenous quarters are one element of Asmara's unique identity: although the city has nineteenth-century characteristics, it is also famed for its abundance of twentieth-century Modernist architecture.

As well as implementing the housing policies that supported and perpetuated the myth of the racial supremacy of Italians, the colonial administration transformed some urban spaces into places for celebrating the strength and supremacy of the Italian Fascist state. Such spaces, including Viale Mussolini, Piazza Roma

and Viale de Bono, were designed to "contain the masses which will celebrate the triumph of civilisation through ceremonial processions, marches and parades".[53] One of the most significant developments in the street layout of Asmara during this short period of unmitigated growth was the establishment of Viale Mussolini as the city's principal thoroughfare and parading ground – literally, for the people, and symbolically, for the Fascist régime. With the Catholic cathedral dominating its central portion, the palm-lined avenue extended from the old Campo Cintato in the west to the Massawa road in the east. Earlier plans by Cavagnari from 1913 had proposed that the future Viale Mussolini should contain a grand oval piazza marking the junction with Mai Bela, but this was never implemented. Cafiero's plan even included the extension of Viale Mussolini right up to the front entrance of the Governor's Palace. Mai Bela's role as a major thoroughfare after it was filled in after 1936 (above left) remained uncertain even in 1937, when the construction of a huge complex, with a hotel and boutique shops, adjacent to the Catholic mission that would have blocked the street completely was proposed (above centre). The project was never approved, probably owing to the need for a south–north arterial road across the city centre.

The three- and four-storey buildings opposite the cathedral were the first large developments on Viale Mussolini, followed by those opposite the theatre between Croce del Sud and the cathedral. Next to the cathedral the striking Falletta building, originally designed in 1937 and altered in 1938, was the last of the buildings to be constructed west of it (see pages 174–75). Further east, beyond Mai Bela and on both sides of the street, rose numerous tall apartment buildings with shops and cafés on the ground floor. On the north side of the street was the striking Cinema Impero with its accompanying bar (see pages 163–65) that with the many shops, restaurants, cafés and bars made this central boulevard the commercial and social hub of the city almost overnight. Although at this time Eritreans could not use these facilities, the custom among Italians for strolling up and down this avenue each evening (the *passeggiata*) was adopted by Eritreans when the city became their own.

LEISURE FACILITIES AND CLUBS

The boom in population resulted in an equally sharp growth in leisure amenities to keep the inhabitants entertained. Before the mid-1930s the only cinemas available to the Italian population included the small Eritreo in the old city centre on the former

One of Asmara's many bars

Design for a restaurant with roof terrace and dance floor

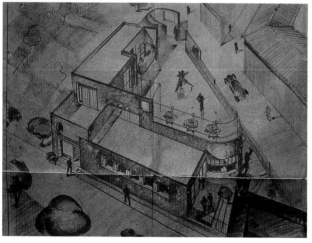

Via Regina; the slightly larger Dante Cinema in the former Via Dalmatia, which still exists; and the cinema in the grounds of the Catholic mission. The arterial road towards Decemhare started at the west end of Viale Mussolini and became one of the city's principal streets. It was named Viale de Bono after the distinguished Italian military general Emilio de Bono, who was Governor of Eritrea for a short period in the 1930s. Cinema Roma, constructed in 1937 halfway along this street, was the first major cinema in Asmara (see pages 161–62). As Cinema Dux (a reference to Il Duce – Mussolini) it had, oddly, been refused planning permission because of its name. Other cinemas followed soon after, including Cinema Augustus, later called the Capitol (see pages 168–69), and Cinema Odeon (see pages 166–67), and many more were proposed but never realized. Cinema Roma, Cinema Augustus and Cinema Odeon all exist

today, with their original fixtures and fittings, exhibiting a wistful aura of a golden age of cinema. A cinema for Eritreans, called Cinema Hamasien, was also constructed (see page 160), while another was proposed (but never built) just outside the Orthodox cathedral (see page 61, top right).

With a notable selection of cinemas, bars, restaurants and even official brothels in Asmara, the Italian population lacked little in the way of evening entertainment. During the day there was an equally broad variety of options: golf courses, tennis clubs, horse racing, athletics clubs, football, a swimming pool, cycling clubs and even motor racing. The former sports stadium on the north side of Viale Crispi that hosted horse racing, athletics and military parades had to be relocated to the north of the city when the land on which it stood was needed for building after 1935. The entrance of the 'new' stadium is one of Asmara's few mildly Art Deco structures (opposite, left).

There were also various unions and social clubs in Asmara, which were extremely popular with the Italians. As in Italy, these associations were often constructs of the Fascist Party and were designed to provide a sense of inclusiveness and participation among all levels of colonial society. The popularity of such clubs and organizations, including those for workers, women, youth and government officials, is indicated by statistics from as early as 1930, which show that of the 4188 Italians in Eritrea at that time, 350 were members of the Eritrean Federation of the Fascist Party, 570 of the Opera Nazionale Dopolavoro, a working men's after-hours club, and 600 of the Opera Balilla, Mussolini's Fascist youth movement. Proportionally there was a much higher membership of such clubs among the Italian population in Eritrea than there was in Italy.[54]

The stadium in Asmara, dating from the 1930s (far left)

Past: the Casa del Balilla (centre left), occupied by the Opera Balilla; and present: the Casa degli Italiani (left)

The buildings occupied by these clubs were also very important as physical representations of the characters and aims of the clubs themselves. The Casa del Fascio, originally built in 1928, was the official headquarters of the ruling party and housed its various clubs (see page 122). It was radically altered in 1940. The Opera Balilla (above centre) occupied the buildings of the present Casa degli Italiani (above right), the gateway of which still bears the Fascist *fasces* emblem on either side of the doorway. This type of overt symbolism, derived from that of ancient Rome, often adorned buildings of Mussolini's period of rule and illustrates an accepted contradiction in Fascism of using references to the past under the pretext of being a modern political movement. As Mussolini's policies became increasingly extreme, so the symbolism became more explicit: such "a surfeit of Fascist signs, images, slogans, books, and buildings compensate for ... its forever unstable ideological core".[55] One of the best examples of the use of such symbolism was the building of the Opera Nazionale Dopolavoro on Viale Giuseppe Garibaldi (see page 64, top left). The *fasces* have since been removed, but the building still closely resembles its original form. Such alterations to many of Asmara's buildings presumably occurred under the British Administration, which attempted to dismantle the physical and intellectual remnants of Fascism.

NEW ARCHITECTURAL STYLES AND THE DEVELOPMENT OF THE MARKET AREA

During the late 1930s, and particularly after the invasion of Ethiopia in 1935, for which Mussolini faced widespread international condemnation, the Fascist Party line became increasingly repressive. In architecture Fascism was beginning to control the creative process, which had previously enjoyed considerably more freedom in Italy than in Fascist Germany. The Italian architect Giulio Pediconi claimed that by 1938–39 there was a change of atmosphere within the architectural world: "All of a sudden these young architects were being told what to build and do."[56] Agnoldomenico Pica, an architect and architectural historian, believed that "under Fascism everybody competed to prove themselves more Fascist than the next ... the anti-Fascist propaganda that followed was rubbish".[57] As the Fascist régime became more dogmatic, so the individuals and groups appearing to oppose it were persecuted. As Gene Bernardini wrote: "Becoming ever more belligerent and doctrinaire after the Ethiopian war, Mussolini struck back at those Jewish organizations abroad that had vigorously protested against Fascist aggression. ... at the same time the Italians had begun to introduce anti-miscegenation laws in Ethiopia to enforce separation of the races."[58] The misery and anguish that this policy caused for Eritreans are well documented, and it remains one of the many distressing chapters in Eritrean history.

As Asmara developed during the late 1930s, however, many new architectural styles replaced the earlier eclecticism or references to historic forms. Far from the motherland, Eritrea provided a perfect environment for innovation and experimentation. There is much evidence to suggest a distinct penchant towards Modernism from the mid-1930s, where before none had existed, though even more radical styling was adopted at the end of the decade. From 1935 to 1941 many buildings were constructed in the Rationalist or Novecento styles or referred closely to them, and equally as many were planned but never built. These buildings ranged from small, single-storey apartments to multi-storey commercial developments.

Past: the Opera Nazionale Dopolavoro building; and present: the office of the National Union of Eritrean Women (right and centre right)

Modern styling appeared in even the most modest buildings (far right)

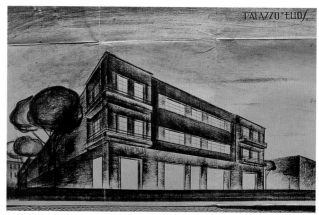

Whether municipal demands drove the tendency towards Modernism or whether it was the preference of the individuals practising in Eritrea cannot be determined. What is apparent is that the period from 1935 to 1941 saw a style that was broadly distinctive from that after 1941, when, as happened after the First World War, there was a reversion to the comfortable familiarity of traditional forms and a search for stability in an unstable world. This change is perhaps unsurprising, since "the spirit of the age" to which Rationalist architecture constantly made reference before 1941 was altered dramatically after Italy's defeat.

Significant developments other than the construction around and expansion of Viale Mussolini markedly affected the character and form of the city centre. The largest of these was the plan by Ferrazza for the redevelopment of the market area, which aimed to beautify this previously disordered area of the city centre by creating a long Romanesque piazza with arched colonnades stretching the full length of the existing market (see pages 128–29). Gardens and fountains would enhance the environment and provide scale to the overall composition. Ferrazza's plans did not stop at the market area. At the eastern end of the market was the old mosque, in front of which, running perpendicular to the market square to the north and south, lay more open spaces ripe for redevelopment. Ferrazza envisaged that both the market and the mosque squares could serve as impressive public arenas linking vast areas of the city centre.

Ferrazza's plans were only partially realized. Work started with the new mosque, built in 1938, which acted as the axis joining both squares. The colonnades on either side of the main building of the mosque provided a pedestrian-only thoroughfare linking

A Modernist former villa, now an office

the market square with the mosque square, known as Largo Libya, which extended as far as Viale Milano (now Afabet Street) in the north of the city. The newly redesigned and cobbled square in front of the mosque featured a central mosaic motif with three *fasces* and the year "XVI". This referred to Mussolini's ambitious and conceited act of renumbering the calendar years from his attainment of power in 1922. The date has since been erased, but the *fasces* still exist. Beyond the mosque square and further to the south are the fish and vegetable markets (top and centre right), designed slightly earlier in an eclectic style fusing Roman and Moorish elements. Doric colonnades skirt the northernmost building, while a large glass-block dome acts as a centrepiece. The extensive open space proposed in Ferrazza's scheme extended even further southwards across Viale Mussolini, but the public gardens and open spaces at that end were never fully realized and were soon swallowed up by buildings, including the monumental municipality building.

In the market area the construction of the colonnades on both sides of the market square began in stages. With the exception of the large two-storey building containing stores, shops and dwellings at the eastern end of the square, behind the mosque (see page 128), the plans for the buildings on either side of the market square remained predominantly unfulfilled. Even as late as the 1950s additions were being made, but the market area remains in a largely muddled and unfinished state. Ferrazza's original plans were rendered mostly obsolete when pedestrian access linking the two squares was sealed off in 1943 (see page 131).

PLANNING AND DEVELOPMENT IN THE HISTORIC CENTRE AND SUBURBS

Another plan for Asmara's open spaces aimed to transform the city's historic heart – Piazza Roma. This public square behind the central post office had been subjected to numerous improvements since its inception in the 1890s. However, in 1937 the municipality received a proposal to convert this area into an underground centre providing telecommunications and secretarial services, and even public baths (see pages 170–71). The elaborate design provided for a public garden and café area at surface level. For reasons unknown the plan was never realized, though it only requires experience of the monsoons to see that such a development could quickly resemble an aquarium. Today Piazza Roma is a car park, a reminder of increasing encroachment by the motor car on civic spaces and the need to protect such historic urban spaces for public use.

Construction of the fish and vegetable markets, with the old mosque still standing in the background

The fish market under construction

The mosque square being laid out in 1938, with the completed vegetable market in the background

Design for a Modern residential
and commercial complex along
Via Regina

Viale Crispi in the 1930s

In and around the historic centre of Asmara (apart from Viale Mussolini) few large buildings were constructed, probably because either the existing ones were adequate or enough open land existed elsewhere for development. Nevertheless, numerous proposals were submitted for the older parts of the city, including several multi-storey commercial and apartment buildings (above left) for the historic former Via Regina. The only large building to obtain planning permission in this historic quarter, besides those on Viale Mussolini, was the Palazzo Minneci, designed in 1939 (see pages 177–79).

Further west on Viale Crispi (above right), the main road leading to the former Fort Baldissera, many new buildings were constructed, since this area of town had been relatively undeveloped up to the 1930s. It comprised, on both sides of the road, the district sandwiched between the Governor's Palace and government buildings in the east, and the former Fort Baldissera and the Queen Elena Hospital below the fort in the west. The exact history of the fort remains unclear, although it is evident that its strategic use for defence was short-lived, since the perceived threat of counter-attack by local forces after the Italians had settled in Asmara never materialized. A large stadium for horse racing, athletics and military parades, together with a tennis club, previously occupied the land to the north of the main road (see page 53, top), but Cafiero's plan for the city had this entire neighbourhood earmarked for housing and government buildings. By the end of the 1930s this grand avenue was something quite different from what had existed there only a few years before. Starting at the government headquarters and the various clubs for government officials, it headed towards the former fort, passing the city's police headquarters, Cinema Augustus and a large building once home to the municipality,

followed by several apartment blocks and further official buildings. A proposal for a multi-storey car park on Viale Crispi was also submitted in an attempt to deal with Asmara's increasing traffic problem (opposite, top).

Along the streets heading south from Viale Crispi, towards the districts of Gejeret and Campo Polo, many small houses, apartment blocks and shops were built. About halfway along these streets is a junction with the central avenue of Viale de Bono, around which several larger buildings were constructed, including the striking Bar Zilli (see page 185). Further south, in Gejeret, were such industrial facilities as the Alfa Romeo office (see page 145) and, slightly further away on the Decemhare road, the Fiat Tagliero petrol station, with its accompanying offices several blocks away (see page 150). Gejeret also provided ample space for housing, though it was never fully utilized until the 1960s, and even this housing then was of the relatively low-density suburban type. In the centre of this suburb, overlooking the district from a hill to the west, stood the new San Francesco church, designed by the architect Paolo Reviglio in 1938 (see pages 138–39). Built in brick and with elements of the Lombard style, the church is similar in appearance to the central Catholic cathedral. Other suburbs similar to Gejeret included Mai Chiot and Gheza Banda to the south-east. The city planners intended such suburbs, designed in vast grid patterns, to accommodate the thousands of new arrivals from the motherland.

Between the city centre from Gheza Banda is the Mai Jah Jah fountain (opposite, bottom), built in a characteristic stepped form with four horizontal elements; around it are pedestrian paths, beautiful gardens, a road and houses beyond (see pages 172–73). Mai Jah Jah lies directly on the axis of Ferrazza's planned

An unexecuted proposal for what
would have been one of the first
multi-storey car parks in Africa

Cross-section of the design for the
multi-storey car park

The interior of Bar Crispi on the
former Viale Crispi (pages 68–69)

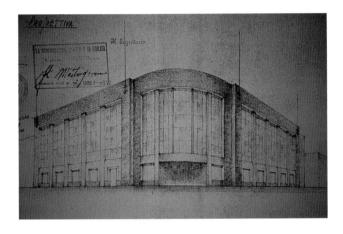

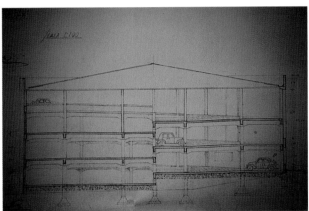

grand boulevard extending southwards from the mosque. An
earlier proposal for the city also indicated an intention to
connect these two important public spaces, which is partially
alluded to in Cafiero's plan but was never fulfilled (Cavagnari's
plans also attempted to link this area to the city centre, by
utilizing an extension of Mai Bela). Between the fountain and the
city centre was a large area of open ground, dotted with small
buildings until the mid-1930s. By the early 1940s this area had
been filled in with housing.

The Mai Jah Jah fountain

DIVERGENT ASMARA, 1941–52

Central Asmara in the early 1940s

In 1941 Italy's dreams of creating a colonial utopia in East Africa vanished for ever when Allied forces entered Asmara on 1 April. As the Italians capitulated swiftly the Allies had no time to organize an adequate administration to oversee the former colony. An Occupied Enemy Territory Administration (OETA) was established and took control in Eritrea, though fighting in the Second World War in Europe was at its peak. As resources were clearly stretched, many Italians retained their posts. In March 1943 the OETA was renamed the British Military Administration, which in April 1949 became the British Administration in Eritrea. Its task was to manage the transition of Eritrea from an Italian colony into a future, as yet undefined, political entity. A number of options were available, all to some extent unsatisfactory at the time: an independent Eritrea, a division of the country between Sudan and Ethiopia, complete appropriation by or federation with Ethiopia, or even an Italian protectorate.

ARCHITECTURE AND INFRASTRUCTURE OF ASMARA UNDER THE BRITISH ADMINISTRATION

When the Allies arrived they were clearly surprised at Asmara's relative grandeur. In a booklet issued by Britain's Ministry of Information, a Mr Dower described Asmara as a "European city of broad boulevards, super-cinemas, super-Fascist buildings, cafés, shops, two-way streets and a first class hotel". However, the disappointing reality beneath the superficial sophistication was evident: he went on to query why the 60,000 Italians could not obtain enough fresh milk, and why vegetables were imported from Rome. His starkest observation concerned, inevitably, the native areas, where 100,000 people "crowded into a latrineless native quarter, which lacked enough water for even their unambitious needs".[59] The difference between the standards of living of the European and native areas was now vast; it would

burden all subsequent administrations and continues to beset the city's planners with problems.

With the Second World War still raging the British were preoccupied with the war effort; architecture and urban planning issues in Eritrea were not as critical as fighting the Nazis in Europe. To British administrators, Eritrea was useful to the extent that it could contribute to that effort. As prisoners of war, skilled Italian workers were forced to assist in the war effort; others, including many Eritreans, manned the workshops and machines that produced valuable components to support the Allied forces.

Urban growth in Eritrea came to a relative standstill. The British policy of making colonies or territories self-sufficient led to the almost complete cessation of expenditure on capital works.[60] Many of the projects proposed by the Italians and due to be implemented during the 1940s were not realized, and those in progress, such as the plan for the market area, were never completed. When the British Administration approved the building of the new premises for the municipality, and the pedestrian walkways on either side of the mosque were bricked up after 1943, the whole of Ferrazza's earlier urban plan was compromised. Additionally, throughout the decade of their control over Eritrea, the British transferred much of the existing industry – factories, machines, components and port facilities – to their other territories to offset the cost of their administration as 'caretakers' of the former Italian colony.[61]

From an architectural perspective the period of the British Administration was marked primarily by the reversion to styles more traditional than the bold Rationalism that had so characterized the late 1930s. Naturally the Fascist symbolism

A building of 1942 in the
Italian vernacular style,
popular after 1941

displayed on many buildings was removed, and it did not appear
on new buildings, but more fundamentally there was an obvious
shift towards rustic styles (top right). Whether, in a world
characterized by instability and uncertainty, many Italians in
Asmara preferred to retreat behind the walls and gateways
of traditional Italian architecture, or whether the architects
themselves were seeking solace in the familiar styles of the
past, is uncertain.

Throughout the early twentieth century the emerging Italian
architectural styles of Rationalism and Novecento were seen as
indicators of progress, reworking and improving previous styles,
and as more progressive than rustic vernacular styles, which
in turn had been regarded by the Fascists as representations
of a distinctive Italian national identity. However, in Eritrea
after 1941 a reversal of this phenomenon occurred. Here the
desire for Italian vernacular was replacing the earlier demand
for Rationalism, a regression similar to that experienced after
the turmoil of the First World War in Italian architecture. It
was a period of confusion, both in society and in the arts.

Design for a building of 1936,
showing the Modern idiom
popular before 1941

One of the leading proponents of the shift from modern to
traditional styles among architects practising in Eritrea was
Roberto Cappellano. His studio in Asmara had produced
numerous designs during the period of the Fascist régime.
These tended to project a bold Modern style, even if the
actual building was diminutive (compare image bottom right
and pages 180–81 with image top right and page 218). After 1941
Cappellano's work reverted to a rustic style, often utilizing the
aedicule (an entrance or covered gateway), which had been
a favourite decorative motif of Novecento. The use of such
devices was intended to generate the feeling of shelter and

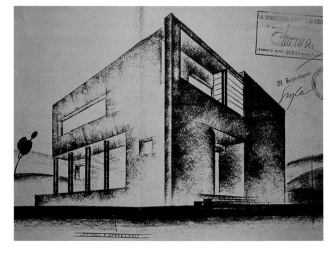

comfort, and on a "deep, primordial level, 'cosiness' and 'security in a hostile world".[62]

THE ITALIAN PRESENCE AND THE MOVEMENT FOR INDEPENDENCE

Although the defeat of Italy in Africa signalled an end to Fascist institutions, many commercial and economic frameworks remained largely unaffected by the change of government for several years. Italian judges still presided in Eritrean courts, Italian tax officers still managed the accounts, Italian law-enforcement officers still remained active in the police, the municipality and all public works were largely under Italian influence, and Italian farmers still worked the land and retained the right to shoot trespassers. The Italian population became slightly smaller in number, though this was inevitable owing to the surrender of the army and the demobilization of personnel employed in the military.

The British Administration was characterized by the emergence of both political movements for and the expectation of full independence, as well as dynamic social and educational programmes. Since there had been enough Italians to fill many of the semi-skilled roles, Eritreans had been banned from attending secondary school under Italian rule. The "Secret School" had been established and run by Wolde-ab Wolde Mariam in the bell-tower of the Evangelical Church in Asmara. Fearing Italian persecution, the school was forced to operate covertly. The British introduced schooling for Eritreans up to the age of eighteen and numerous vocational courses. By 1954 one hundred primary schools and two secondary schools had been built. An active press was established, with newspapers in Tigrinya, Arabic and English; all levels of education were now open to Eritreans; and a new labour movement began to lobby for workers' rights. In 1949 the inequities of a wage system that paid Italian labourers much more than their Eritrean colleagues led to a thirty-seven-day strike from 4 March to 11 April, paralysing the transportation system. The many workers of mixed Italian–Eritrean origin received slightly better pay than the native Eritreans but less than the Italians. Administrative justice, fair pay and abolition of racially discriminatory laws became contentious issues as the Eritrean population started to voice its grievances.

One incident that resulted from this inequality illustrates how racial laws were impracticable. One morning in 1943 Eritrean workers arrived early for their bus to work on the outskirts of Asmara and occupied the seats designated for Italians. Arriving late the Italians noticed that there were no places for them to sit and demanded their seats. A serious argument broke out, and the matter was referred to the local British administrator, Mr Peacock. He explained that while such laws still existed the British were powerless to withdraw the Italians' 'right' to a seat. However, he suggested that the Eritreans organize their own bus service. The Eritreans promptly set about collecting enough money to buy a used truck, and furnished the back of it with wooden benches. Mr Peacock swiftly issued their licence. The Italian bus owner, deprived of much of his source of income, was unable to continue operating his bus service and was forced eventually to sell his bus to the very people he had refused to allow to sit in it. The Eritrean workers became proud owners of a proper bus and, most importantly, could sit wherever they wanted.[63] Several other Italian-owned transport companies in Keren, Massawa and Decemhare also changed to Eritrean ownership around this time.

DORMANT ASMARA, 1952–91

An elaborate tomb in the
Italian cemetery

In 1952 Eritrea was federated with Ethiopia under a United Nations agreement heavily influenced by extraneous issues. The agreement denied Eritreans political independence and led eventually to a devastating period of isolation and destruction in the region. Although Asmara experienced limited expansion during the first years of Ethiopian occupation, two factors led gradually to the decline of urban development: a complete lack of investment and actual removal of some industries by the government of Emperor Haile Selassie, and political oppression by the military régime that deposed the emperor in 1974. Eritrea was annexed by Ethiopia in November 1962, but the war for independence had already begun on 1 September 1961. Spanning four decades, it destroyed both Eritrea and Ethiopia physically and economically, and drew both the United States of America and the Soviet Union into conflict against a relatively tiny but oggedly resolute band of Eritrean guerrilla fighters who eventually emerged victorious.

THE IMPERIAL RÉGIME

The 1950s and 1960s saw some significant development throughout Eritrea, as Haile Selassie attempted to appease the Eritrean population by building a limited number of key public works, such as churches, mosques, schools and hospitals. However, such building took place against the backdrop of the deliberate dismantling of Eritrea's industrial capacity that had already begun under the British Administration, albeit for different political and economic reasons.

Under Haile Selassie's régime the Americans established a base in Asmara, called Kagnew Station, in 1953. It was a multi-million-dollar complex designed for the American National Security Agency. 'Kagnew' means 'to be vigilant' in the Amharic language, and the name was given to both Haile Selassie's father's horse and the Ethiopian battalion sent to fight in the Korean War. The base was situated on the hill once occupied by Fort Baldissera, though a little further south, adjoining the Italian cemetery, in the former Piazza d'Armi. It remained almost entirely isolated from the city until it was closed in 1975 by the Communist régime. American ordnance-survey markers are still visible around Asmara.

In 1965 Queen Elizabeth II inaugurated the redevelopment of the municipality building (see pages 202–04), which included the creation of the vast banqueting hall at the rear of the building. A third storey was added later, and the central tower was heightened. To honour the visit the emperor renamed the former Viale de Bono, one of the city's main thoroughfares, Queen Elizabeth II Avenue. Almost all the street names in Asmara were changed during this period, as the memory of Italian colonization was replaced by Ethiopian rule. This makes orientation in Asmara quite problematic, since some street names have changed up to four or five times simply to satisfy the whims of various colonial rulers or administrators.

During the 1960s a significant number of villas were built on the open land in and around Gejeret and Gheza Banda (see page 229) to house the officials working for the imperial régime, and others who benefited from it. The distinctive style of many of these villas, dominated by diagonal lines and triangular patterning employed both aesthetically and structurally, contrasted dramatically with the strong horizontal and vertical detailing characteristic of Classical and Rationalist buildings throughout the city. Some construction on a larger scale was also undertaken in the city centre, especially towards the eastern end of the main boulevard, formerly Viale Mussolini, renamed Corso Italia during the British Administration, and later Haile Selassie I Avenue by the Ethiopian régime. One very large block, housing apartments and shops, stood next to the Cinema Impero (see page 225) and another on the corner at the south-east end of the avenue (see page 224). A smaller building next to the law courts housed the Bank of Ethiopia.

Following the prevailing trend of 1950s and 1960s architecture, several high-rise buildings were proposed for Asmara, some of which were to be located in the city centre and were as much as fourteen storeys high. Such plans were never fulfilled, with some notable exceptions, including the Nyala Hotel, some distance from the centre, and the Ambassador Hotel opposite the Catholic cathedral (see page 226). Fortunately, the lack of development during this period allowed Asmara to retain its modest, balanced urban scale.

THE COMMUNIST RÉGIME

In Ethiopia in 1974 the Communist despot Mengistu Hailemariam deposed the autocratic Emperor Haile Selassie. As the emperor was losing his grip on power, Eritrean guerrillas had managed to encircle their capital city but were forced to make a 'strategic withdrawal' in 1978, despite having been so tantalizingly close to victory. Mengistu's military régime, more brutal than the imperial one, instigated a policy of ruthless repression, forcing the guerrillas to retreat to the almost impenetrable hills of northern Eritrea, where they dug in until the end of the war. Under the Communists the residents of Asmara faced brutal subjugation and became victims of countless atrocities, including mass murder and terror campaigns.

They also suffered from widespread hunger and extreme shortages of water, fuel, medical care and other basic amenities. The influx of large numbers of army personnel into the cities, and the military government's policy of nationalizing land and property, led to considerable displacement of the population, disintegration of society, serious overcrowding and a shortage of housing. Urban development stalled, which led to congestion, while the existing stock of buildings and infrastructure deteriorated through lack of maintenance. The only significant architectural development under the military régime was the construction of one half of the appropriately monolithic concrete stadium at the eastern end of the former Viale Mussolini. Designed as a vast parade ground for glorifying the military régime, the project was never completed, leaving a vast wasteland opposite a single bank of seating that blights the cityscape to the present day (see page 231).

To the rest of the world, Ethiopia was in a state of civil war, but for Eritrea the war was a matter of survival in pursuit of the inalienable right of self-determination. While Westerners enjoyed the economic boom that marked the 1980s, their only understanding of the plight of millions of people in the Horn of Africa came through pictures on their television sets of skeletal figures starved by famine. Such images spurred a group of pop stars into producing a Christmas record, 'Feed the World', and organizing a concert held in London's Wembley Stadium in aid of famine relief in Ethiopia. However, the world's media, while providing confrontational images of the starving, failed to scrutinize the causes of such horror. Eritrea's plight went unrecognized, and so it was left to fight unaided in a long and costly war, which finally ended in 1991.

INDEPENDENT ASMARA, 1991–2002

Liberation celebrations on
Harnet Avenue

The struggle for independence ended in 1991. Following a referendum, Eritrea was officially declared an independent state on 27 April 1993. Eritrea emerged into a world that bore no resemblance to the one in which it had been created one hundred years earlier. Miraculously, no major battles had occurred within the built-up area of Asmara during the war for liberation, and there was no visible bomb damage. Nonetheless the landscape of the whole city was one of decay and disorder: scenes of boys and girls carrying barrels of water on improvised carts, military ramparts on top of apartment buildings, and bricked-up windows with broken glass and barbed wire fortifying residences facing the street are still vivid in the minds of residents of Asmara. The euphoria of victory did not remove the foul smell from clogged sewage, and the many beggar women

and children indicated widespread poverty. Many colourless, decaying buildings attested to the neglect and destruction of the years of Ethiopian occupation. The basic infrastructure of Asmara was largely in need of a complete overhaul.

ISSUES OF REBUILDING AFTER INDEPENDENCE

Nevertheless, liberation from foreign rule and the prospect of a life of peace and freedom infused all Eritreans with the hope of future development. They set about rebuilding their country with the passion and zeal that had won them independence. Although difficult, the task of rehabilitating Asmara was undertaken with a sense of responsibility, because it was the capital city of a country for which so many had fought and died.

The pressing need for development of Eritrea's towns and cities, including its capital, required careful decisions, and aroused much interest and concern locally and internationally. Some called for the complete removal of colonial buildings, as had happened elsewhere in post-colonial Africa, while others recognized their beauty and durability.

It would have been a bitter irony for Asmara to survive fifty years of neglect only to be destroyed by a decade of new development, but this scenario came close to being realized in 1996 in an incident that illustrated perfectly the determined yet liberal attitude of Eritreans. A renowned German architectural firm commissioned to design the headquarters of the national Bank of Eritrea suggested that the most prestigious location for the building was the site in front of the Catholic cathedral. A grotesque fourteen-storey glass building with numerous smaller structures around it, occupying four blocks of historic Asmara, was proposed. The central building was to be the tallest in the city, towering over the campanile of the cathedral. Before the bank could be constructed the building occupying the site would have to be demolished (see page 125), but when the plans for this move were made public a group of Eritreans protested vehemently. What was it that made these Eritreans so doggedly determined to save this old building? It was the notorious former Italian prison, 'Caserma Mussolini', housed within the army barracks, and the members of this group of ardent conservationists were former inmates!

PROBLEMS OF ENVIRONMENTALLY INSENSITIVE DEVELOPMENT, AND THE CREATION OF THE HISTORIC PERIMETER

The headquarters of the national Bank of Eritrea was not the only modern development proposed for the city. In a period of heightened enthusiasm for progress, it is easy to see how and why such proposals were accepted. However, several buildings were erected without prior consideration for the environments in which they are located. One such example is Nakfa House (above), which dwarfs one of Asmara's most curious examples of Modernist architecture, the Fiat Tagliero service station, and reduces the area around it to a disorientating small space. The building blocks the view southwards from the city centre along Sematat Avenue (*sematat* in Tigrinya means 'martyrs'), and hinders the flow of pedestrian traffic. Other examples of misguided development include the high-rise Blue Building, near Nakfa House; the Housing Bank of Eritrea, at the east end of Harnet Avenue (formerly Viale Mussolini); and the building

of the Red Sea Corporation, in the south-east of the city's historic centre. Such developments attest to insensitive planning born perhaps more out of financial motives than from a genuine concern for the social and environmental aspects of the city's fabric.

In a relatively short time Asmara has also been significantly transformed as a result of the construction of several residential buildings and complexes, most of them on a scale conflicting with that of the existing townscape. Many of these projects have been implemented as a result of *ad hoc* decisions, in an attempt to alleviate the shortage of housing. Even though they have contributed to reducing some housing problems, they have a negative impact on the city's environment. The implications for Asmara of increasing the city's housing stock by means of such large-scale projects as the Sembel Housing Complex, Space 2001 and Kushet Housing without an overall city plan or urban design guidelines must also be considered carefully.

Asmara's significance as a centre of early twentieth-century architecture cannot be overstated. Debates concerning the course of future development in Asmara persist, with mounting pressure for improved living conditions, better commercial facilities and more housing. Asmara faces a seemingly insoluble problem: how to provide for the needs of a growing population in an area rich in history and therefore requiring preservation. In a country as keen to develop as Eritrea, it is important that the cost of development does not outstrip the value of what might be lost in the process. It is essential that Asmara's exceptional heritage is preserved for the benefit of its own population and for present and future visitors, and that the will and commitment to undertake co-ordinated action prevail. Herein lies a vital test for such organizations as the Cultural Assets Rehabilitation Project (CARP) and other municipal and governmental institutions.

In 2001 a historical perimeter was formally established in Asmara, encircling an area of about four square kilometres (one and a half square miles), or 4% of the total area of the city. This area contains the city's historic centre and the majority of its architecturally and historically significant buildings that need protection from unwarranted modifications. Following the preparation of detailed guidelines and regulations, new buildings within the historic perimeter will have to meet stringent criteria that aim to ensure that the integrity, harmony and scale of Asmara's unique urban environment are preserved, while the city's natural growth can continue unhindered.

FUTURE ASMARA

The skyline of Asmara, from left to right: the spire of the Protestant church, the minaret and domes of the Grand Mosque, the campanile of the Catholic cathedral and the tower of the Orthodox cathedral

Today the urban population of developing countries is growing faster than the rural population, and within twenty years more than half the people in Africa will live in cities.[64] Most urban dwellers in developing countries live in conditions of 'housing poverty', *i.e.* without adequate shelter or provision of such basic infrastructure as piped water, sanitation, drainage and waste disposal.[65] Moreover, the rise in extreme poverty, although a global phenomenon, is occurring mainly in sub-Saharan Africa.[66] It is against the background of the growing global polarization of rich and poor that poor countries such as Eritrea are attempting to improve their situations. As a capital city and the largest urban centre in Eritrea, Asmara has to fulfil various social, economic and political functions. The actions taken today regarding such functions will determine the city's potential to participate in and benefit from the global economy in the future.

USING ASMARA'S HISTORIC ARCHITECTURE AS A FOUNDATION FOR FUTURE DEVELOPMENT

Although a policy of racial segregation prevailed during much of the period of Asmara's development, it should not be forgotten that an evidently attractive and functional urban environment with integrated and wide-ranging activities was created – even though only a limited section of society benefited from it at the time. This came about through a conscientious concern for public buildings and spaces, and a measured approach to urban planning. Within the European zones of the city, this environment grew through the careful planning and siting of parks, piazzas, fountains, wide pavements, and various forms of vegetation and decoration. This successful approach (obviously without the policy of segregation) should not be discarded just because it has colonial associations. That all the citizens of Asmara now share the outcome of this urban experiment should be regarded as the ultimate success of independence over iniquitous racial segregation.

Additionally, Asmara has the advantage not only of having been spared the negative developments inherent in poor planning in its earlier history but also of being able to learn from the mistakes experienced by other cities. Overcoming contemporary urban problems with the benefit of hindsight is critical if the city is not to fall prey to the irresponsible planning and decision-making that have so blighted cities in the rest of the world. Ensuring, therefore, that future developments in Asmara incorporate those aspects that have made it so cherished should be a priority. Short-sighted opportunism must not be allowed to jeopardize sustainable long-term growth. Awareness of the unconscious proliferation of new forms of segregation, such as those related to income, social status and access to transportation and opportunities, is also important.

The greatest challenge facing Asmara was, and still is, how to expand in a manner that responds to the real needs of its inhabitants. The legacies of Italian colonialism and Ethiopian occupation are complex: the city is a composite landscape of different physical and social environments that have been superimposed on one another over the last 110 years. The different layers of this landscape raise many issues regarding housing needs, rehabilitation of existing infrastructure and provision of new, delivery of social services, conservation and economic growth.

POVERTY, HOUSING PROBLEMS, POPULATION GROWTH AND WATER SHORTAGE

The physical structure of Asmara reflects the typical colonial partition of urban quarters into 'European' and 'indigenous', the result being that a large part of the city still lacks basic infrastructure and services. With many of Asmara's inhabitants living in squalid conditions, it is evident that poverty is one of the foremost problems in the city and will remain so for some time. Addressing the issue of poverty requires a clear recognition of and consensus on priorities, and an appropriate vision for urban development. It is widely recognized today that the best way of fostering prosperity is to encourage the sustainable development of human settlements.[67] The present trend towards urban sprawl in Asmara, caused by and related to the use of private motor cars, will not lead to sustainability, either environmentally or socially. The majority of the housing plots within the city have been allocated to those on high incomes, but alternatives to single-plot housing should be considered in order to achieve optimum population density.

The war of liberation left a legacy of poverty, disruption of society and deterioration of the built environment, exacerbated by the latest border war (1998–2000) as many deportees from Ethiopia and people forced from their homes in the border region migrated to the capital city. The contemporary trend towards urbanization suggests that such migration from rural to urban environments will continue. A town-planning committee established in 1998 determined that by the year 2015 the population of greater Asmara would reach about 600,000. This statistic includes the population of thirteen small villages, as the committee forecast that some 8000 hectares (19,800 acres) of

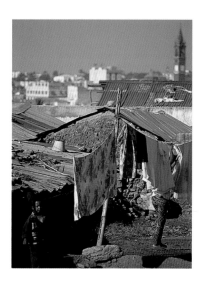

The deprived areas of Asmara's northern suburbs

rural land would be developed. Already the population of Asmara comprises more than half of the nation's total urban population. The challenge of population growth, even with a modest rate of increase, is daunting.

Asmara has always been a compact city, contained in an area of about eighty square kilometres (thirty square miles). It measures no more than eleven kilometres (seven miles) across, which means that all significant areas are within reasonable walking distance of one another. This distance is expected to grow to twenty-five to thirty kilometres (sixteen to eighteen miles), but inevitably the city will continue to sprawl into the rural hinterland. Journey times to work and school will increase, putting pressure on the already stretched transportation systems. Distribution lines for water and electricity will also need to be extended.

Availability of water is another critical factor. The potential capacity of existing water sources is 41,000 cubic metres (53,300 cubic yards) per day. The rate of water loss in the distribution system remains critically high. Compounding this problem is the inevitable increase in the number of houses receiving running water as a result of other infrastructure improvements, resulting in rising rates of consumption. At present the connection rate stands at 60% of households, with the other 40% relying on delivery of water by tanker. As the demand for running water increases, sources further afield will need to be tapped, and delivery and distribution costs will rise beyond the means of the majority of Asmara's citizens. So critical are these concerns that the town-planning committee of 1998 concluded: "Water supply will be the critical deciding factor for the development and expansion of Asmara."

Poverty, water shortages, housing shortages and endemic environmental problems already confront the city. Dealing at the same time with issues relating to Asmara's historic urban areas is a daunting task that will require great assistance from domestic and international agencies. Only by the observation and understanding of what already exists will it be possible for the city to grow in a manner that reconciles equity, economic growth and efficiency. Future preservation and development initiatives should be founded on an inclusive, participatory mandate, encouraging Asmara's citizens to take joint responsibility with the government for regeneration and sustainability. The international community is also being encouraged to learn about and participate in the regeneration of Asmara so that visitors and locals can enjoy it now and into the future.

This book sheds some light on the key factors that have shaped the remarkable city of Asmara throughout its long, fascinating and often tragic history: destruction and construction, survival and loss, great achievements and deplorable neglect, personal hardship and collective joy, a unique mix of local and international influences, and the appalling consequences of racism and political oppression on indigenous, egalitarian socio-cultural traditions. No nation or city on this planet, however ancient its origins, is immune from external influences, evil or virtuous, that have helped shape its physical environment and its cultural, religious and social traditions. Most of the construction of Asmara occurred during a dark period of international history, and some of its buildings were direct constructs of sinister forces. Like so many nations, Eritrea was forced to make colossal sacrifices in order to secure the inalienable right of self-rule in a wider, global community.

Harnet Avenue

While architectural styles come and go and political movements rise and fall, the physical evidence left by any political régime is likely long to outlast the ideology of its creators. The act of construction, however it is driven, is profoundly different from that of destruction. It remains, therefore, for future custodians of the heritage to utilize architectural legacies in ways that support and uphold the values of Eritrea, which have been often born out of surmounting past difficulties. Thousands of Eritrean labourers toiled in the construction of Asmara, while others lost their lives defending a régime about which they knew little or perhaps for which they cared little. Asmara fared poorly after the Second World War, but after independence it is Eritreans who are rejuvenating and restoring it. Asmara has survived. In return for drudgery and sacrifice alone, Eritreans have more than earned the title of 'custodians of Asmara'. Asmara is a uniquely Eritrean city, and the preservation and sustainable development of its undeniably important urban heritage rest with the need for good governance, and will remain a major responsibility.

NOTES

1. Cogliati 1901, pp. 34–35.

2. Denison and Paice 2002, p. 17.

3. Pankhurst 1985, p. 68.

4. Beckingham 1954, pp. 182–84.

5. Bizzoni 1897, p. 199.

6. Cogliati 1901, p. 28.

7. In the Tigrinya language the word *geza* is used to describe a group of dwellings.

8. Some ambiguity once existed over the meaning of the name Asmara, since early Italian accounts suggested incorrectly that it means 'little rains'.

9. R. Pankhurst, *Economic History of Ethiopia, 1800–1935*, Addis Ababa (Haile Selassie I University Press) 1968, p. 693.

10. Barrera 2003.

11. *Ibid.*

12. This predicament has been widely documented, but for a succinct account read Tekeste 1987.

13. Rainero, 'I Primi tentative', p. 57. Cited in Tekeste 1987.

14. Barrera 2003.

15. F. di Stefano, 1897, in Gresleri, Massaretti and Zagnoni 1993, p. 145.

16. Martini to MAE 26/04/01. Archivio Martini, Archivio Centrale dello Stato, busta 4, Rome.

17. Cogliati 1901, pp. 26–27.

18. *Askari* (singular *askaro*) was the name given to Eritrean soldiers fighting in the Italian army.

19. Cogliati 1901, pp. 32–33.

20. Federzoni to Mussolini, 'SE Federzoni Luigi (colonie, affari generali)', 24 November 1926. Archivio Centrale dello Stato, Segreteria Particolare del Duce – Carteggio Riservato, b. 23, f. 224, Rome. Cited in Barrera 2003.

21. Paoli 1908, p. 54.

22. Cogliati 1901, p. 30.

23. Paoli 1908, p. 55.

24. Preface by Bertram Grosvenor Goodhue in A. Whittlesey, *The Minor Ecclesiastical, Domestic and Garden Architecture of Spain*, New York (Architectural Book Publishing Co.) 1917. Cited in Etlin 1991, p. 129.

25. Zagnoni, in Gresleri, Massaretti and Zagnoni 1993, p. 150.

26. Onnis 1956, pp. 186–97.

27. Cogliati 1901, p. 132.

28. Mussolini 1935.

29. Etlin 1991, p. 23.

30. M. Piacentini, 'L'Esposizione d'architettura a Lipsia', *Annuario d'Architettura*, Associazione Artistica fra i Cultori d'Architettura in Roma, 1914, p. ix. Cited in Etlin 1991, p. 53.

31. Mezzanotte 1921, p. 299. Cited in Etlin 1991, p. 189.

32. Etlin 1991, p. 212.

33. *Ibid.*, p. 198.

34. *Ibid.*, p. 445.

35. De Martino and Wall 1988, p. 52.

36. Etlin 1991, p. 445.

37. *Ibid.*, p. 384.

38. 'Communicato M.I.A.R. n. 4', 26 January 1931, in M. Cennamo (ed.), *Materiali per el'analisi dell'architettura moderna. Il M.I.A.R.*, Naples 1976, p. 98.

39. 'Manifesto' of the Second Italian Exhibition of Rational Architecture, in Cennamo (ed.), *op. cit.* note 38, pp. 103–04.

40. Etlin 1991, p. 387.

41. Soffici, 'Periplo dell'arte'. Cited in W. Adamson, 'Ardengo Soffici and the Religion of Art', in Affron and Antliff 1997, p. 65.

42. Castellano, 1948, states that the population of Asmara in 1939 was made up of 53,000 Italians and 45,000 Eritreans, p. 539.

43. Governo Generale dell'Africa Orientale, Stato Maggiore, *Il Primo Anno dell'Impero*, Addis Ababa 1938, I, p. 44.

44. Cogliati 1901, p. 33.

45. For more extensive insights into the policies regarding *askari*, see Tekeste 1987 and Barrera 2003.

46. Barrera states: "Concubinage with local women was widely practiced by Italians of all walks of life." Barrera 2003.

47. De Angelis 1921, pp. 65–73.

48. All these quotationss are from the 'Piano Regolatore di Asmara-Relazione Cafiero', ACS–MAI, busta 106, Rome. Cited in Locatelli 2001.

49. A. Teruzzi, 'Le opere pubbliche', *Gli Annali dell' Africa Italiana*, IV, no. 2, 1939, p. 391. Cited in Locatelli 2001.

50. Gresleri, Massaretti and Zagnoni 1993, p. 201.

51. Bertarelli 1929, p. 624.

52. Gresleri, Massaretti and Zagnoni 1993, p. 201.

53. 'Piano Regolatore di Asmara-Relazione Cafiero', *op. cit.* note 48.

54. Governo dell'Eritrea, Segreteria del governatore, *Notiziario politico Eritrea-Etiopia*, no. 3, March 1930, p. 2; Archivio storico diplomatico del Ministero affari esteri (Rome), ASMAI, 35/1, f.3. Cited in Barrera 2003.

55. Schnapp 1992, pp. 1–37.

56. Giulio Pediconi was a partner in the Rome-based Paniconi Pediconi architects. De Martino and Wall 1988, pp. 74–75.

57. *Ibid.*, p. 76.

58. G. Bernardini, 'Anti-Semitism', in Cannistraro 1982, p. 29. Cited in Etlin 1991, p. 570.

59. G. Dower, *The First to be Freed*, London (Ministry of Information) 1944.

60. Trevaskis 1977, p. 45.

61. Pankhurst 1952, p. 13.

62. Summerson 1963, pp. 2, 23. Cited in Etlin 1991, p. 198.

63. Memher Yeshak, Eritrean teacher.

64. United Nations Centre for Human Settlements 2001.

65. United Nations Centre for Human Settlements 1996.

66. Castells 1998.

67. United Nations Centre for Human Settlements 1996.

THE BUILDINGS OF ASMARA

1899–1935

FORMER GOVERNOR'S PALACE GROUNDS

Original name Governor's Palace Grounds (1889–1952); Imperial and Presidential Palace Grounds (1952–91); National Museum (1991–97)
Current address Denden Street
Original address Viale Crispi
Date 1889–1921
Map reference D6/D7/D8/E6/E7/E8

The grounds of the former Governor's Palace were one of the first sites settled by the Italians in Asmara, in 1889. Near the first Italian military encampment on the Plain of Asmara, where the Government Headquarters now stand, the former Governor's Palace and the surrounding offices of the early colonial administration were close enough to the camp to benefit from its protection, yet far enough from it to enjoy the isolation provided by the extensive woods and gardens. The site has witnessed several changes throughout its relatively long history, but has remained at the heart of state affairs, both literally and metaphorically. The area is dominated by the former Governor's Palace, the Neo-classical façade of which flaunts the authority of its resident from the end of a long avenue leading directly to the entrance gate. An urban plan from the Fascist period indicates that this grand entrance was intended to be the end of the main Viale Mussolini (now Harnet Avenue). The plan was never realized, and the entrance remains hidden discreetly behind a public park. Several buildings within the grounds are notable both architecturally and historically. Some date back to the earliest Italian settlements in Asmara, while the late Emperor Haile Selassie of Ethiopia added others as recently as the 1960s.

Government office

Original name Comando Presidio
(Office of the Local Commander of Asmara)
Architect unknown
Date 1889–95
Map reference D7/E7

One of the first buildings erected by the Italians in Asmara, this wood and brick structure with a tin roof remains in very good condition. In an early Italian travelogue its curious style was described as 'equatorial', *i.e.* resembling the British and French colonial architecture of the tropics. With a simple and symmetrical structure, the building has a raised veranda and a diminutive upper storey. It shared the palace grounds with other buildings in a similar style, one of which is identical to it (see below).

Building under renovation
Original function first Governor's Palace
Architect unknown
Date 1889–95
Map reference E7

Identical to the former Comando Presidio, this building was once the Governor's Palace and the residence of the first civilian governor, Ferdinando Martini. After the completion of the new palace it became a guesthouse for visiting dignitaries.

President's Office

Original name Circolo Ufficiali (Officials' Club) (1889–1921); Segreteria e Gabinetto (Office of Secretary and Ministry) (1921–41)
Architect unknown
Date two separate buildings built between 1889 and 1895; later destroyed and replaced by a single building in 1921
Map reference D7

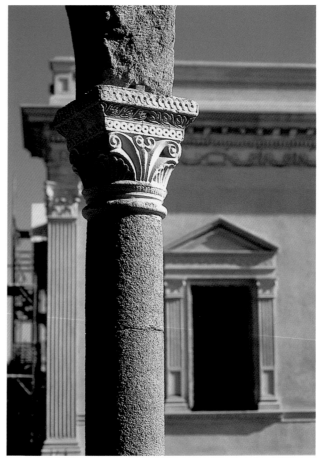

On the site of this neo-Gothic office built in 1921 once stood two smaller buildings housing the offices of the first colonial administration in Asmara. Constructed from brick and wood, but only one storey high, the earlier buildings were of a similar colonial style to that employed in the first Governor's Palace and the Comando Presidio. The 1921 building is more substantial. A symmetrical, single-storey structure composed of a central entrance flanked by two wings, the building is constructed with a deep course of lightly rusticated stone below a course of brick in which are set distinctive neo-Gothic windows and stone blocks arranged irregularly. Decorative motifs, such as patterned plasterwork and iron fleurs-de-lis, appear on some of the exterior walls, all of which have decorated and painted plaster friezes beneath wooden eaves supporting a slate roof.

State Palace

Original name Governor's Palace
Architect unknown
Date 1905
Map reference D7/E7

Set among exquisite gardens and built on a steep slope, this bright-white structure is fittingly grandiose for its use as Eritrea's primary state building. The symmetrical façade, with decorated architrave and cornice, pediments, window pediments, and pilasters mounted on each corner, is undisputedly Asmara's finest example of the Neo-classical style. Having moved the official capital of the colony from Massawa in 1900, Governor Martini commissioned the palace as his official residence and as a setting for state functions. P. Gandolfi & Co. completed the work by 1905. An earlier design for the palace in a Moorish style was reputedly favoured by many in Rome, but under Martini's orders the design was changed to a Neo-classical one. Owing to the gradient on which the palace is built, the basement that once housed the kitchens, storage rooms and servants' quarters opens to ground level at the rear, where Emperor Haile Selassie's favoured architect, Arturo Mezzedimi, designed and built a concrete staircase in the 1960s.

A majestic entrance of Grecian Corinthian columns supporting a pediment provides access to Asmara's most formal interiors. Ornate frescoes and stucco plasterwork with floral motifs and the crest of the Italian royal family once decorated the palace's enormous rooms. Some of these were painted by Francesco Saverio Fresa, an Italian artist who arrived in Eritrea in 1916 and completed a number of commissions during his years there, including work for some monasteries and the Asmara Theatre. After extensive alteration the interior now bears scant resemblance to the original. Mezzedimi transformed much of the palace and other buildings in the grounds during the late 1960s. A private cinema, additional state function rooms and private rooms, an external double staircase, lavatories and bathrooms altered the arrangement of the building, particularly in its western range, though the façade has remained almost entirely intact. Interior frescoes were altered to accommodate various symbolic

motifs such as the Lion of Judah and the Menelik Star, which have since been replaced.

After independence the palace, its grounds and all the buildings therein became the home of an impressive national museum, and, for the first time, these interiors were open to the public. Since 1997 they have undergone extensive renovation, which will enable them to be used again as official state function rooms. The renovation programme has tried where possible to return the interiors, fixtures and fittings of the palace to their original state.

Guard's House

Original name Posto di Guardia
Architect unknown
Date unknown
Map reference D7

Small but significant, the neo-Gothic guard's house stands at the entrance to the Governor's Palace grounds, in front of the Government Headquarters. The building is a curious arrangement of Gothic forms and motifs, of which there are three key elements. The most striking is the small two-storey tower at the south-east corner of the main building, with its tracery on the first floor. This simple window consists of three foils piercing a neo-Gothic spandrel, supported by two slender mullions. The largest element, the part of the building to the right of the tower, is of a similar style to the larger offices inside the grounds, with neo-Gothic windows, open brick façade and decorated architrave. This might suggest that this building was constructed at about the same time, around the early 1920s. Like the small tower, it is topped with a pitched slate roof. The third key element, a small colonnade of Gothic arches, skirts the south and west walls of the main building, providing shade and completing the overall composition.

GOVERNMENT HOUSE

Original name Palazzo del Comando Truppe Coloniali
Current address Denden Street
Original address Viale Crispi
Architect unknown
Date 1910s
Map reference D8

Overlooking Asmara from its elevated viewpoint in the heart of the administrative district, the Government House has always represented authority. The building stands in a central position, at the south end of the former Campo Cintato; facing south at the junction of the central thoroughfares of Harnet Avenue, Denden Street and Sematat Avenue, it affords spectacular views across much of the city. Little is known about its exact origins, though the site on which it stands is that of the first Italian settlement. It is said to have been constructed in 1915 and designed by Odoardo Cavagnari, though the evidence for this is so far inconclusive.

Many later alterations have transformed this once modest government office into the present monumental block. Originally it was a bright-red symmetrical two-storey building (top right), with an extra wing on the ground floor, set behind a grand double staircase with an ornate balustrade and surrounded by well-maintained gardens and trees. Simplified Neo-classical motifs, including pilasters and window pediments, adorned the façade, composed of a vertically arranged central portion containing the main entrance, a formal first-floor window with a balcony, and a decorated pediment in front of a slightly pitched slate roof. On each side of the entrance two rooms on the upper floor were aligned with two of the three rooms below. The roofs of the third room at either end of the ground floor provided first-floor terraces. All windows were rectangular with plaster surrounds and pediments, but curiously the openings on the ground floor were arched.

During the 1930s an extension incorporated both ground-floor terraces, making the building a solid form. Further extension on three of the building's axes was completed during the reign of Haile Selassie. The new elements retained the styling employed in the original design, though the façade was simplified and a cornice added to conceal the roof. The consolidation of the covered terraces on both wings provides additional room space, albeit to the detriment of the aesthetics of the façade, further undermined by the use of aluminium rather than wooden window frames. A reorganization of the space around the building, including vehicular access to the rear, has allowed some semblance of the gardens at the front to be retained, but the sheer scale and dominance of the altered structure prevents the creation of the intimate atmosphere afforded by the original greenery on this hill.

FORMER LORENZO TAZAZ STREET

Original function shops and apartments
Current address 175-11 Street
Original address Via Martini
Architect unknown
Date early 1900s
Map reference D8

Situated at the heart of Asmara's historic quarter, 175-11 Street once formed part of the main road traversing the Plain of Asmara in the 1890s. The street, climbing gradually from north to south, was the only interruption to the road's straight course from the edge of the escarpment, leading down to Massawa in the east and to the Italians' primary defence post, Fort Baldissera, in the west. The former Campo Cintato behind 175-11 Street was responsible for this slight diversion since the steep sides of the hill on which the camp was situated made it an impractical obstacle to traverse. As the camp provided security, the city's first businesses were established along this short section of the road; they included cafés, a club, tobacco shops, barbers' shops, paper shops and printing shops. In 1906 one traveller to Asmara said of this street that "it lacks nothing", but expressed disgust that the annoying sound of a gramophone resonated from one café! Behind this street the city centre, containing the former Piazza Roma and the central post office, developed.

Two buildings, each in a distinct style illustrating the diverse approaches of Asmara's early builders, dominate the eastern side of the street. Although they are among Asmara's oldest buildings, the exact date of their construction is not known. The building to the north is distinctly Classical and typically Italianate, with a long balcony in front of the three windows on the upper floor (opposite, top left). Of particular note are the plaster mouldings, including the military crest set in an open pediment above the central window (bottom left). The deliberate emphasis on vertical alignment of the building's key elements starts at the floor with each doorway, and is continued by the mouldings below each balcony bracket and above each window, below the eaves. The balcony is also divided by balusters, adding to the vertical emphasis, and Art Nouveau-style decoration features on the railings. The central window is distinguished by a slight protrusion of the balcony and the obvious grandeur of its mouldings. The symmetry of the building is broken only by the slight incline of the street.

The building to the south is distinguished by the lancet arches that form the windows and the decorative frieze. These features owe more perhaps to Moorish styling than to Gothic, as is also indicated by the ornate and beautifully decorated rear window, comprising a circular element with an ogee arch and filled with coloured glass (far right). Nevertheless, the overall style of the building is eclectic, with a variety of decoration used throughout, including the fine door handles, marble staircase, Classical-style pilasters, original glass and iron canopy, and original interior fittings; these last, including the fine wooden cabinets in the shop, are among the most well-crafted and the best-preserved in Asmara.

Immediately behind these two buildings a vegetable market once thrived in a small square, which was later built over. A saddler's shop was among the numerous concerns to have occupied these buildings, though today one is home to the Bini group of businesses, which include photography, shoe-making and import/export, while the other contains a number of apartments. During the Ethiopian occupation the street was renamed Lorenzo Tazaz Street, after the Eritrean diplomat who presented the Ethiopian case to the League of Nations in response to Italian aggression in the 1930s.

ALBERGO ITALIA

Original name Albergo Italia
Current address Nakfa Avenue
Original address Corso del Re
Architect unknown
Date 1899
Map reference D8/D9

Located on the north side of the bend in the main road as it ascends the hill on which the Campo Cintato was located, the Albergo Italia is one of Asmara's oldest surviving stone buildings. Built in 1899, it was the first hotel in Asmara and has remained among the city's most important hotels. Architecturally it is not a remarkable building, but it displays several interesting details, such as the interior balcony with three round arches and the plaster crest on the exterior. Its most significant feature, however, is the old dining-room, quite unlike any other room in Asmara. With its original ornate plasterwork in the form of fruit, flowers, fish, figurines, faces, and ornamental urns on pedestals, this room remains one of the city's historic gems. An enormous bunch of plaster roses tops the cast-iron column in the centre of the room, a feature that appears in many of Asmara's oldest buildings.

Proposals by the architect Ugo Dal Mas to redevelop the hotel in 1936 would have increased its height from two to three storeys. The plan was never realized, and the building has remained largely the same since it was constructed. However, it has recently undergone comprehensive restoration and modernization of its interiors. Having been named the Keren Hotel for several decades, the hotel will assume its former name of Albergo Italia.

POST OFFICE SQUARE

Original name Piazza del Tribunale; later Piazza Roma
Current address Nakfa Avenue/175-10 Street
Original address Corso del Re
Date 1890s–1910s
Map reference D9

Central post office administration

Original function tribunal, treasury, and post and telegraph office
Architect unknown
Date 1900–06
Map reference D9

Constituting Asmara's civic centre, the Post Office Square remains a vital component in the city's historic fabric. Established within easy reach of the military camp, and later the focal point of the grid system employed by the city's planners at the end of the nineteenth century, the square was soon the hub of commercial activity in Asmara, with the first banks, post office, shops and hotel nearby. The square has served various purposes, though it was most famously a public park with a large fountain in the centre. During the 1930s an ambitious plan was proposed to build a subterranean complex underneath it (see pages 170–71), but instead the square became a car park and sadly has remained as such. However, several national banks and the central post office occupy historic buildings of varying importance, dating from the turn of the nineteenth century, around the square.

Dominating the south side of the square is the grand 'palace' of the former tribunal, which also housed the treasury and the post office (left). Now it is home to the administrative offices of the central post office, which was housed in an extension to the south side of this building. At ground level is a distinctive Roman-arched portico, filled in at either end. Above this rises a façade of simplified Neo-classical elements, with an old Milanese clock at the top set in an arched relief below a Classical pediment edged with dentils. Inside, a fine stone staircase with curled wrought-iron railings in a vaguely Art Nouveau style leads to the offices on the upper floor. The exterior, once bright white, has now been painted green.

Central post office

Original function central post office
Architect Odoardo Cavagnari
Date 1916
Map reference D9

To meet the increasing demands on the postal service of the Italian population in Eritrea, the post office was extended in 1915. The extension, completed the following year, consists of a single-storey building attached to the south side of the tribunal. Counter service is provided in the main hall, with the counters and post-office boxes around the walls behind an Ionic colonnade, which supports a raised roof with windows in each of the arches between the columns. These windows are composed of a central circle surrounded by twelve smaller circles, positioned like the digits on a clock face.

Perhaps the most interesting of the post office's features are the decorative frescoes in the atrium depicting aspects of farming and forestry in the various regions of Eritrea (bottom left). Each of the country's sub post offices is named in a garland in the frieze below the coffering. Painted decoration of Roman artefacts also embellishes the frieze on the building's exterior. The entrance has bold rusticated stonework, with a Greek pediment above, decorated with dentils and once filled with a plaster crest. Beneath the pediment is the sign in Tigrinya, Arabic and English for the central post office.

Commercial Bank of Eritrea

Original name Office of the Eritrean Salt Company
Architect unknown
Date 1910s
Map reference D9

On the eastern side of Post Office Square the imposing former Office of the Eritrean Salt Company looms three storeys high. Its style is indistinguishable from that of the colonial architecture produced by other Western European countries, although such elements as the arched reliefs, balcony and irregular proportions of the window openings appear rather awkward in the overall composition. Once occupied by the Military Union and the Fascist Youth Movement, the building became the home of the Banco di Roma. In 1937 the architect Roberto Cappellano submitted a design (unexecuted) for modernizing the building.

Bank of Eritrea

Original function unknown
Architect unknown
Date 1895–1905
Map reference D9

At the north-west corner of Post Office Square is the distinctive Bank of Eritrea. The history of this building is uncertain, as one early record from 1906 describes it as the Albergo Italia (the hotel one block to the west), while in the 1920s it was identified as the Café Roma. The building was the earliest on Piazza Roma, and clearly reflects the Moorish styles that inspired the Italians after they arrived in Massawa around this time. What is certain is that by the late 1930s it was the Banca d'Italia. It was later a police station under the Ethiopian regime, before becoming the headquarters of the Bank of Eritrea after independence. The building is one of Asmara's finest examples of neo-Gothic architecture, with the style once being described as influenced by Venetian architecture. The symmetrical façade is composed of three elements: two brick wings – with pointed-arch windows on the ground floor and rectangular ones on the upper floor – frame the entrance, the portico and gallery of which both have three arches.

University of Asmara Training Centre

Original function bank
Architect unknown
Date 1915
Map reference D9

Tucked discreetly into the south-west corner of the former Piazza Roma, now Post Office Square, the ornamental façade of the University Training Centre is one of the few in Asmara that could claim some allegiance to the neo-Baroque style. Both external walls have simplified Doric colonnades that converge at the corner of the building, which has been made into an elaborate entrance with a sweeping double staircase, a rounded portico with a saucer-domed roof, and a decorative pediment. Ornamental balustrading runs along the bottom of the colonnade (and continues down the staircase), while a patterned frieze and entablature adorn the top. A plaster eagle once stood above this, but has since been removed.

FORMER ADUA SQUARE

Original name Piazza Italia; later Piazza Michele Bianchi
Current address Nakfa Avenue/Keren Street
Original address Corso del Re
Architect unknown
Date 1910s–20s
Map reference C10/D10

Following the implementation from 1913 of extensive town-planning projects by the city's new Civil Works Office, headed by the renowned architect and engineer Odoardo Cavagnari, the street plan of much of downtown Asmara took the form of a grid system. The new plan centred on the former Corso del Re, which was eventually superseded by the thoroughfare to the south now known as Harnet Avenue. In the centre of Corso del Re, Cavagnari planned a piazza, similar to what was then the Piazza Roma further west, on the north side of the road and near to the huge market one block to the north.

The first building to be constructed, in 1916, was on the north side of the square. Standing on a slight slope descending from east to west, the building was Classical in style, with its façade divided into three distinct sections. Rounded and triangular pediments crowned the windows on the first floor, with the central window having a balcony. Similar decoration adorned the doorways below. After 1922 an identical building was constructed on the west side of this earlier building, thereby lengthening the façade. The uses of the building are now partly residential and partly commercial. On the east side of the square are two slightly later buildings, also

both now divided between residential and commercial use (opposite, centre right). That to the north has a simple Classical façade but interesting interior decorative features, such as floor tiles, ceiling ornament and a frieze in the Art Nouveau style. The date of construction of this building is not known, though it is certainly of the same period as its neighbours. The southernmost building, constructed in 1922 on the corner of the square adjoining Corso del Re, has an equally noteworthy interior but a more distinctive exterior, featuring lion-shaped brackets below the balconies and the rather grotesque cherub-face motifs above the windows. The overall appearance comprises a curious mix of styles, with hints of neo-Baroque ornamentation and Art Nouveau ironwork on the balconies.

REGIONAL OFFICE OF MINISTRY OF EDUCATION AND OFFICE OF FINANCE POLICE

Original name Office of Economic Affairs and Office of Mining and Technical Services
Current address Beleza Street/Bihat Street
Original address Croce del Sud/Via G. Sapeto
Architect unknown
Date 1915
Map reference E8

The second building (above right) is equally curious, but for different reasons. The plain, symmetrical façade is dominated by the patch stonework, further accentuated by painting the stones black and the mortar white. Highland Eritrea has a wealth of stone suitable for construction, including granite and lignite, and these are commonly utilized for buildings in Asmara, including this one. Stepped plasterwork frames the ground-floor windows, while flattened or broken pediments, derived from certain forms of traditional French architecture, crown the first-floor windows.

Although two of Asmara's lesser-known historic structures, these buildings – of the same date but clearly different in style, scale and form – were among the first two-storey buildings south of what is now Harnet Avenue. The plot that they occupy, between the high ground on which the European villas are situated and the shallow valley beyond which lie the grounds of the former Governor's Palace, is awkward terrain on which to build as it has a steep gradient.

On the smaller of the two buildings (above left), typically eclectic in style, the Classical pediments above the front entrance and window, the faux-rusticated plasterwork and the overall asymmetry of the lower half of the building appear out of place against the simplified detailing employed throughout the upper part of the façade. The brackets supporting the entablature and the protruding podium in the centre of the cornice disrupt the composition further. The simple interior, with scant decoration, provides adequate and well-ventilated office space as a result of its high ceilings.

ASMARA THEATRE

Original name Teatro Asmara
Current address Harnet Avenue/Beleza Street
Original address Viale Mussolini/Croce del Sud
Architect Odoardo Cavagnari; Aldo Vitaliti and Pietro del Fabro
Date 1919–20; renovated 1937
Map reference E9

Probably the last work of Odoardo Cavagnari (1868–1920), one of Asmara's foremost engineers and the chief of the Civil Works Office from 1913, the Asmara Theatre was the city's first purpose-built venue for the performing arts. Standing at the crest of Harnet Avenue, and one of the largest buildings in Asmara at the time of its construction, the theatre once dominated the city centre. It was designed in 1919 and completed in 1920 as a joint venture between the Società ARPA (Anonima Ritrovi Pubblici Asmara) and Dita Dilsizian Freres of Milan. Original planning permission had been granted on condition that a restaurant and tennis courts should also be built on the site, but the liquidation of its sponsors in 1924 meant that the project was never fully completed, as evidenced by unfinished brickwork at both ends of the portico. The government acquired the undeveloped land but sold it in 1927 to Società Fratelli Ingegneri, which in 1937 constructed a series of buildings, including a dancehall and shops, in front of the theatre at street level, and adapted the theatre itself into a cinema. The cinema operated until 1957 when it was sold to Haile Selassie's son-in-law, who was the emperor's representative in Eritrea. Today the building functions as a theatre again, though it is awaiting urgent renovation and modernization.

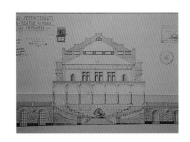

Constructed in reinforced concrete faced with brick and plaster, the symmetrical façade has elements from an assortment of styles, including the Romanesque and Renaissance. The most striking is the portico, formed of seven Roman arches supported by slim Ionic columns. Above the portico is a gallery, access to which is through two arched doorways, one on either side of the building, on the upper floor. Two elegant, sweeping staircases leading from either end of the main entrance portico descend to street level. Gardens featuring a large concrete shell fountain and decorative flowerbeds extend in front of the theatre. From the west the visual division of the building into three separate components – from north to south, the reception area, the auditorium and stage, and auxiliary space for storage and back-stage offices – can be better understood. The side wall itself exhibits an extraordinary mixture of styles and has a notable external walkway for private access to the gallery.

In the reception area are the ticket booth and a bar, both added when the theatre was converted into a cinema. Supported by square concrete pillars, a gallery runs around three sides of the room. Next to two doors providing access into the auditorium are the stairways to the balconies and boxes. Approximately 750 people can be seated in the theatre. Above the stalls is a large saucer-dome ceiling decorated by Francesco Saverio Fresa (who also painted frescoes in the former Governor's Palace), with a circular fresco of eight dancing women in a frame depicting eight peacocks (opposite, bottom). The design of the fresco, which remains in very good condition, appears to have been influenced by the Art Nouveau style. Fresa also painted a large fresco of a dancing Eritrean woman in the arch above the proscenium, but this was removed, perhaps during the late 1930s.

Architects Aldo Vitaliti and
Pietro del Fabro carried out the
renovations to the theatre in 1937.
The conversion of the theatre into
a cinema resulted in an awkwardly
positioned projection box in the
upper balcony, but the most
significant alteration was the
construction of a series of shops
and other buildings at street level
in front of the theatre. A series of
round-arched openings, two to the
east and three to the west of the
theatre entrance, provided access
to additional retail, office and
recreational space. Today the
Telecommunications Centre
occupies the former dancehall, the
flat roof of which prevents further
beneficial utilization of the grounds
around the theatre, especially on its
western side.

REGIONAL GOVERNMENT OFFICES

Original name Commissariato dell'Hamasien
Current address Eritrawit Ade
Original address Piazza Victor Emmanuel III
Architect Paolo Reviglio
Date 1920
Map reference E10

One of the most important buildings in Asmara before the city's rapid development in the 1930s, the Commissariat was the seat of the former municipal and regional authority of Hamasien. Romanesque and Renaissance styling similar to that on other buildings of this period, such as the theatre, the Catholic cathedral and the original Casa del Fascio, has been employed here. The building stands imposingly (though now slightly concealed by palm trees) in front of a picturesque public garden, below and to the north of the site of the former camp of the infamous tribal leader Ras Alula.

The two wings of this symmetrical building protrude only slightly and are more ornate than the central part, which includes the entrance with a small stairway leading up to it and a balcony above. The walls are divided into three distinct horizontal elements: irregular stone patterning at the base, brickwork from the window-sills on the ground floor up to the bottom of the window arches on the first floor, and a pale stucco and lightly diamond-patterned frieze above the brick course. In the central portion the brick stops at the sills of the first-floor windows. The eaves on the wings are vaulted in a similar manner to those on the theatre and the original Casa del Fascio. All windows have round arched openings, though the windows in the wings are divided into three by slender mullions supporting solid spandrels of decorative stonework.

CATHEDRAL AND COMPOUND OF THE CATHOLIC MISSION

Original name Cattedrale e Missione Cattolica
Current address Harnet Avenue/176-17 Street
Original address Viale Mussolini/Mai Bela
Architect Oreste Scanavini
Date original 1895; reconstructed 1923
Map reference D9/D10

In Eritrea, Catholicism preceded the arrival of the official Italian state administration by several decades, as a mission had been established in the northern town of Keren. Almost immediately after General Baldissera occupied the Plain of Asmara in August 1889 a Catholic mission was founded on a small site to the west of Campo Cintato. It later occupied a vast area on the western banks of the Mai Bela River, to the east of Campo Cintato and directly north of Ras Alula's fort. The mission began on a small scale on the second site, with just a few buildings around the first

Catholic church of St Mark the Evangelist, built in 1895 in the Lombard style and consecrated in 1897 (top right). The church, simple in form, painted white and with an accompanying bell-tower, was small, but deemed more than adequate for the modest needs of the Catholic population of Asmara at the end of the nineteenth century. The surrounding buildings evolved over the years to include a nursery school, an elementary school, a printing press, a priest's residence, a library, a Capuchin convent, and even a cinema and theatre. One early traveller felt that more

attention had been paid to prayer than to aesthetics: "Dominating all the city, rises the Catholic Mission, which to tell the whole truth, is of poor appearance and of bad architecture" (Renato Paoli, *Nella Colonia Eritrea*, Milan [Fratelli Treves] 1908, p. 56).

As the population of Asmara grew steadily it was clear that the church would not be sufficient for the burgeoning Catholic population. The decision was taken to pull it down and replace it with a grand cathedral, which took two years to construct and was finished in 1923.

The adjoining campanile was completed by 1925. The new cathedral, with a distinctive plain brick exterior in a style emulating the architecture of Lombardy in northern Italy, like that of the first church, was to dominate the town.

A series of steep steps from what became the main street in Asmara leads to the entrance – a large arched doorway set beneath a tall, mullioned lancet window that dominates the south wall. Above the point at which the nave and aisles, separated by round-arched arcades, adjoin the transept is a large eight-sided dome painted a vivid sky blue and decorated with gold stars. A figure of an angel cast in bronze stands atop the dome; like that of the bells in the campanile, the bronze was obtained from Austrian cannons seized after the Battle of Carso in 1917. The interior features numerous frescoes with quotations and depicting angels, cherubs and other religious figures and scenes, the most elaborate of which is in the apse: the Ascension of the Virgin Mary, by an Italian painter, C. Maratti. Decorative

combinations of brown brick and pale stone with various carved motifs and details are also used, for example in the four squinches below the dome. The altar is made of white marble. Many fine details, both architectural and historic, appear in the church, not least of which are the tomb of the first apostolic vicar in Eritrea, Camerata Carrara, and a plaque on the north wall dedicated to the benefactors who assisted in financing the building of the cathedral, including one Benito Mussolini. Above is a huge decorated wooden ceiling with wide, elaborately patterned trusses.

Behind the church is a large courtyard, in which stands the soaring campanile, built in the same brown brick that was used to construct the cathedral and

many of the outlying buildings, as well as many villas in the town built during this period. These bricks came from the first Italian brickworks in Eritrea, established by the Italian entrepreneur Colongo Modesto. At over 50 metres (160 feet) in height the campanile remains the tallest structure in the city, affording superb views of the surrounding area. On each of the four sides is a clock face, above which hang the bells. Beyond the immediate environs of the church lie the buildings of the mission school, in the north-west corner of the compound; the printing press, in the south-west corner, which used to print sacred and scholastic texts in the local languages of Tigré and Kunama, and the ancient language of Ge'ez; the priest's residence, to the west of the cathedral; and the convent of the Capuchins, to the east.

MEDEBER MARKET

Original name Caravanserraglio
Current address Qelhamet Street
Original address Via Ual Ual
Architect Odoardo Cavagnari
Date 1914
Map reference A12/A13

Caravanserraglio is an Italian translation of an old Turkish word meaning 'caravan enclosure'. These stopping-points on the caravan routes provided facilities for repairs, stocking up on supplies and trading goods. The market's present name, Medeber, is an Arabic word describing the same facility. The Caravanserraglio was a vital element of Asmara for traders travelling from the coast into the hinterland and further afield into Ethiopia and Sudan.

The original location of the Caravanserraglio was due east of the city, just south of the railway station on the banks of the Mai Chiot, a tributary of the Mai Bela River, next to Asmara's former clay-pigeon shooting club. Following the implementation of the new urban plan initiated by the Head of the Office of Civil Works (Ufficio Centrale del Genio Civile), Odoardo Cavagnari, in 1913, the Caravanserraglio was moved into the new industrial area in the north-east corner of Asmara. Cavagnari designed the new buildings for this facility, which included a weighbridge, offices and clinics. Gradually the Caravanserraglio

changed from a stopping-off point for travellers to a centre for trading goods, especially textiles. By the 1950s it had developed into a manufacturing facility where local craftsmen produced all manner of items, often using recycled materials, from ovens to grave heads made of metal. The demand for such items – and thus the manufacture of them – increased as imported items became scarcer. By this period many of the original buildings had been destroyed – either through neglect or by a fire that ravaged the market in 1958 – leaving only the smaller premises around the perimeter wall and the characteristic entrance gateway, with its distinctive tower, that originally had administrative and medical offices on either side.

The concrete structure, faced in brick and stone, is simple and symmetrical in form, while the tower, composed of three slender rounded archways, provides an unmistakable landmark. A pediment above the tower appears to have once contained a clock, though there is little evidence of it today. The outer buildings now house many manufacturing workshops and chilli-pepper mills (centre), brought together from various sites around the city by the mayor in the 1960s.

HAMASIEN HOTEL

Original name Albergo Hamasien
Current address Beleza Street/171-10 Street
Original address Croce del Sud
Architect Paolo Reviglio
Date 1919
Map reference F8

By order of the government of the Italian colony, the Hamasien Hotel was constructed in 1919 and opened in 1920 as one of Asmara's leading hotels. Situated on the western edge of the Quartiere dei Villini, the heart of Asmara's early European civilian settlement, the hotel sits on the crest of a small escarpment that descends sharply to the west and thereby commands excellent views of the city in all directions. The peculiar pyramid-topped tower, evocative of an Alpine chalet, makes the Hamasien Hotel one of Asmara's more curious buildings. Architecturally it is not of outstanding quality, but its unique form adds to Asmara's rich mixture of architectural styles. It has remained a hotel for most of its existence, though it briefly housed the headquarters of the British Military Administration during the 1940s. In 1965 another hotel, the Ambasoira, was built next door; the two are now jointly managed. Today the Hamasien Hotel is in poor condition and requires urgent restoration.

IBRAHIM SULTAN SECONDARY SCHOOL

Original name Martini High School and Gymnasium
Current address Beleza Street/Berasole Street
Original address Croce del Sud/Via Piaggia
Architect unknown; Aldo Fornaini
Date 1920s; 1964
Map reference E9

The Ibrahim Sultan Secondary School, situated at the north end of Beleza Street, is easily recognizable from its west entrance owing to its commanding position and distinctive turquoise colour. The building has always housed a school, though the Fascist Culture Club (Circolo di Cultura Fascista) also had its headquarters here until 1929, presumably before it moved into the Casa del Fascio on Harnet Avenue (then Viale Mussolini). The original structure built in the 1920s had only one floor of classrooms, but a second floor was added in 1964 by the architect Aldo Fornaini. With windows identical in form to those of the original building, this extension is sympathetic to the original architect's design.

The building is in a Neo-classical Modernist style and is notable for its simplicity of form. The main entrance, located to the left of the three arches on the west-facing wall (top left), is recessed behind trees and shrubs, which are also used in the inner courtyard to provide an attractive and tranquil space inside the building compound (bottom left). The line of arches on the south side of the school building can be compared with the more simplified version on the south side of the fish market designed by Ferrazza. Series of arches, fewer in number, are also used on the front entrance and in the courtyard.

VILLAS AND OFFICE OF MINISTRY OF WATER RESOURCES

Original function villas
Current address Beleza Street/Bihat Street/Maryam Gmbi Street
Original address Croce del Sud/Via G. Sapeto/Via Oriani
Architect Paolo Reviglio; unknown
Date 1910s
Map reference F8 and E9/E8/E6

Numerous small villas around
Asmara dating from the first two
decades of the Italian occupation
are quite distinct from the simpler
single-storey buildings more
common in the European quarters
of the earlier colonial period. Built
in a medieval style, with various
Romanesque references, these
later villas are characterized by a
greater use of surface detailing and
decoration, which includes the use
of arched windows, mullions and
patterned friezes. They tend to be
two storeys high, but the second
storey often consists only of a
single room in the form of small
tower. Typical construction
techniques include a lower course
of irregular stonework, with a brick
or plastered course and a decorated
frieze above. Brickwork laid in
various geometric patterns is
used for decorative effect.

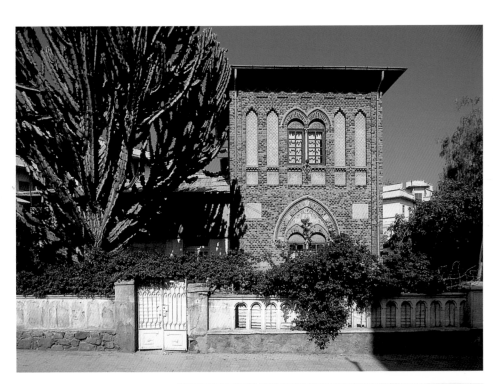

These traditionally styled buildings were almost all intended for residential purposes, though the third example (opposite), despite its attractive façade, has a rather sinister history. Built by an Italian, it was originally a villa nicknamed "the castle". The owner applied to have it extended to incorporate a dancehall, though whether this application was successful cannot be determined. However, it does appear to have been extended at some point in its early history; the wing to the south may be one such addition as it is in a different style from that of the rest of the building. During the Ethiopian Dergue régime the villa was appropriated by the government and converted into the most feared prison in Eritrea. Political prisoners were held in tiny cells at the rear of the building and routinely tortured. The dunking well, torture chambers and whipping post still exist as testaments to the atrocities that political activists fighting for an independent Eritrea had to endure. The building is now occupied by the Ministry of Water Resources.

VILLA QUARTER

Original name Quartiere dei Villini
Current address area bounded by Harnet Avenue, Beleza Street, 173-5 Street
and Bdho Avenue
Original address area bounded by Viale Mussolini, Croce del Sud, Via Pellegrino
Matteucci and Viale Giuseppe Garibaldi
Architect various (unknown)
Date from 1910s
Map reference E9/F9

The European residential quarter developed in the Italian colonial period remains an anomaly in Asmara, a stark contrast to the unpretentiousness of the 'native' quarter and to much of the residential housing in the downtown district. Its grandiose villas, set among sumptuous gardens filled with flowers, shrubs and trees, once accommodated Asmara's elite. Of the many villas in the area, the most notable are probably the peculiar two-storey towered villa, formerly home to the manager of the Bank of Rome (top left); the former municipality building (top right, centre and bottom left), with its elaborate ironwork; the former Villa Spinelli, built by a local Italian businessman (opposite, top), and the former residence of the mayor; and the residence formerly of the viceroy and now of the Italian ambassador (opposite, bottom left and right). Each has a distinctly individual style, perhaps because they were constructed at a time when eclecticism was the dominant trend in architecture in Asmara, *i.e.* before 1936.

It is difficult to say which of these four villas is the oldest, as dates of construction are uncertain. Many other residences in this quarter are single-storey, and are some of Asmara's earliest permanent dwellings, dating from the end of the nineteenth century. In the 1930s a change in the building regulations stipulated that all new residential buildings in the city centre must have at least two floors. In 1936 a second storey was added to the former Villa Spinelli, a single-storey building that had been on that site for many years. The former viceroy's residence was also extended in the same year. The other two villas, two storeys high, remain in their original form and are in need of restoration.

1935–41

MINISTRY OF EDUCATION

Original name Casa del Fascio (Fascist Party Headquarters)
Current address Harnet Avenue/Keskese Street
Original address Viale Mussolini/Via Gustavo Bianchi
Architect unknown; Bruno Sclafani
Date 1928; extended 1940
Map reference D9/E9

Perhaps the most austere of Asmara's buildings, the former Casa del Fascio is a fine example of monumental Fascist architecture. The evolution of the building corresponds to the increasing severity of the ideology of the Fascist regime from the 1920s through to its eventual defeat in the early 1940s. The first Casa del Fascio, which began as a social club for party members, was built in 1928, one block east of the similarly styled theatre (opposite, top). Set back from the main road, the building was entered up two flights of stairs that led to a quatrastyle portico, the pediment above which appeared to indicate a dedication to Benito Mussolini's brother Arnaldo, reading: "Casa del Fascio – Arnaldo Mussolini." The portico, acting as a physical and symbolic link between the party and the people, provided a platform from which speeches could be delivered to the masses gathered below at street level.

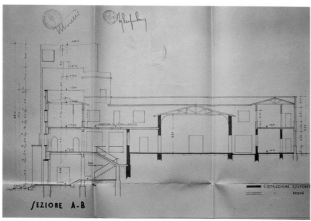

SEZIONE A-B

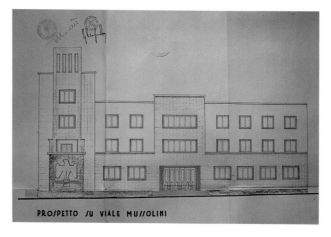

PROSPETTO SU VIALE MUSSOLINI

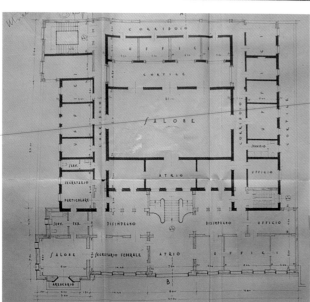

The entrance opened almost immediately into the main assembly hall (see page 124, centre), the walls of which were once covered with fine examples of traditional 'Abyssinian'-style paintings, regrettably destroyed before independence (see page 124, top). Depictions of the Queen of Sheba and Solomon; the legend of the serpent that is said to have shaped the Eritrean and Northern Ethiopian highlands; elephant, giraffe and lion hunts; St George and the dragon; and the construction of local churches all decorated the walls, while in the crescent-shaped vaults were paintings of allegorical figures of animals in the Byzantine style.

The symmetry of the building's façade, its overall style and its elevated height above street level lent it a certain authority, but this was evidently not explicit enough for the Fascist regime in its later years. In 1940 a modern façade designed by Bruno Sclafani was added to the older building, an act that was clearly driven by political ideology rather than pure practical necessity. The monumentality and boldness of the new design, with its soaring tower and the massive scale of its frontage, is formidable, demonstrating figuratively the power of the state. The street and building are no longer separated by staircases, vegetation and decorated walls, but are now thrust together, symbolically uniting the party with the people. Photographs from this period illustrating the building's construction suggest that it was probably not finished in time to be used as intended, since the Allies arrived in Asmara in 1941.

The massive asymmetrical façade is composed of several elements, the most imposing of which is clearly the tower, itself symmetrical in form (see page 122, bottom). At the base of the tower is a huge vacant space upon which a sculpture of the Fascist eagle was intended to hang, though it appears that this scheme was never realized (see page 123, right). Above the space for the eagle is a balcony from which Mussolini, if he had ever come to Eritrea, would almost certainly have made his speeches. The vertical alignment of the elements is emphasized by the vertical arrangement of three square windows set in a chamfered frame, with three horizontally aligned lancet windows above, themselves framed in the top of the tower. The main body of the building is composed of three blocks, each distinguished from the others by a different surface finish, though the whole is integrated visually through vertical and horizontal alignment of the windows. The dominant block is formed by the central section and ground floor, which meet at the entrance, and is different in colour and texture from the upper storeys on either side of the entrance. These side elements contain the windows for the first and second storeys, though that to the left of the entrance, being half the length of the other, contains half the number of windows. The steep incline of the street on which the building was constructed does not allow for a symmetrically aligned building of this scale (unlike the municipality building, see pages 202–04), which may be why the architect deliberately designed an asymmetrical structure.

FORMER BANK OF ERITREA

Original function army barracks
Current address Harnet Avenue/173-5 Street
Original address Viale Mussolini/Via Pellegrino Matteucci
Architect unknown
Date 1935–36
Map reference D9/E9

Once the Agricultural Office of Eritrea, this was one of Asmara's first Modernist buildings. With its refined Classical style and emphasis on geometric simplicity, it is a fair example of Novecento architecture. Set back from the street, the building is surrounded by open space, which with trees and shrubs provides an attractive setting. The entrance, set at an angle of 45 degrees to the rest of the building, and with seven slender windows set above the doorway, has been treated differently from the side walls, which are characterized by the simple vertical alignment of their elements.

The building has served a number of very different functions: as a military prison, as the British police headquarters and latterly as a bank. After independence in 1991 it was due to be demolished to make way for a vast new complex of glass high-rise buildings proposed by a German architectural consultancy. Such was the enormous scale of the project and so evident its disregard for the historic architecture in the centre of Asmara that the outcry from local Eritreans, including former prison inmates, caused it to be shelved. This incident also led to greater awareness of the need to preserve other historic buildings in Eritrea.

125

GARAGE

Original name City Sanitation Office
Current address Massawa Road
Original address Massawa Road
Architect unknown
Date approximately 1938
Map reference (off the map)

This building, situated over a kilometre (almost a mile) from the city centre, once housed the City Sanitation Office. It successfully provides both office space and vehicular access: the entrance and exit are set below the clock tower, with an internal passageway linking the offices on either side of the central part of the building. The simple arrangement and alignment of the wings, which have seven evenly spaced square windows on the ground floor and just two on the top floor, and are constructed in bare brick, are clearly inspired by Rationalist thinking.

However, the eye is always drawn back into the centre of the building, with its projecting tower, and to the large, protruding semicircular balcony above the entrance and exit. Besides the obvious aesthetic departure from the simple style of the wings, the central part of the building also has a different surface treatment of painted plaster. In addition, there would have once been a central column of light from the ground to the top of the tower, projected through the glass panelling that has since been removed. At ground level the original guard's office has been cleverly and inconspicuously incorporated into the overall design.

MINISTRY OF HEALTH

Original name Colonial Police Headquarters
Current address Denden Street/172-5 Street
Original address Viale Crispi/Via Sarone Franchetti
Architect unknown
Date approximately 1938
Map reference D5

Another good example of Novecento styling, the present Ministry of Health – previously occupied by, among others, the colonial police headquarters and an eye hospital – has a distinctive concave façade. It is unclear why the architect chose this shape, although early street plans for the junction on which this building stands proposed the creation of a circular piazza by erecting four buildings with concave façades. This plan was clearly never realized. A similar but more overtly Classical building was proposed in 1943 for what is now Harnet Avenue, but was never built.

The building exhibits a strong vertical emphasis through the alignment of the windows and their surrounds, formed by simplified pilasters, on the three upper floors. Each first-floor window has an independent balcony, further accentuating the unbroken vertical alignment of the building's elements. On the ground floor the windows are restricted in height, providing limited visibility to the street, though still aligned with those above. The doorways, also aligned with the windows above, are positioned at the centre of the concave façade.

MARKET

Original name Piazza Italia
Current address Decemhare Street/Barentu Street
Original address Piazza Italia
Architect Ferruccio Mazzanti (1941); Giuseppe Arata (1942); Guido Ferrazza
Date 1938–52
Map reference C9/C10/C11/D11

The area around the market square had always been used by Eritreans for trading all manner of produce from around the region (top right). As such, it had encouraged many people – not only Eritreans but also Italians, Jews, Greeks, Muslims and Coptic highlanders – to settle in Asmara, evidence of which was provided by the many rows of *agdos* constructed northwards from the market until the 1930s. The market square quickly became the hub of commercial activities as well as an important social gathering place where Italians, Eritreans and others would mix freely. Its importance in the latter regard cannot be overstated, since in Eritrea, uniquely among European colonies, this racial integration evolved naturally rather than artificially. By the time Mussolini's racial law was imposed in 1938, the market area was considered socially and physically unacceptable by the Fascists; it was deemed 'untidy', and its function as a meeting point for different races was fundamentally opposed to Fascist policies of segregation. In reality the Fascists could do little to amend this situation significantly.

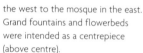

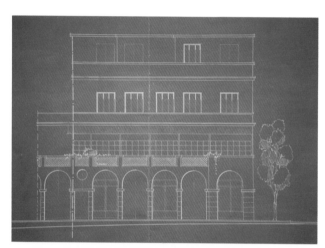

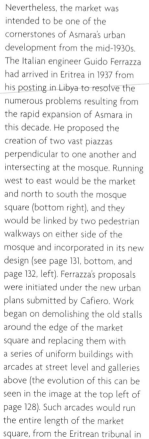

Nevertheless, the market was intended to be one of the cornerstones of Asmara's urban development from the mid-1930s. The Italian engineer Guido Ferrazza had arrived in Eritrea in 1937 from his posting in Libya to resolve the numerous problems resulting from the rapid expansion of Asmara in this decade. He proposed the creation of two vast piazzas perpendicular to one another and intersecting at the mosque. Running west to east would be the market and north to south the mosque square (bottom right), and they would be linked by two pedestrian walkways on either side of the mosque and incorporated in its new design (see page 131, bottom, and page 132, left). Ferrazza's proposals were initiated under the new urban plans submitted by Cafiero. Work began on demolishing the old stalls around the edge of the market square and replacing them with a series of uniform buildings with arcades at street level and galleries above (the evolution of this can be seen in the image at the top left of page 128). Such arcades would run the entire length of the market square, from the Eritrean tribunal in

the west to the mosque in the east. Grand fountains and flowerbeds were intended as a centrepiece (above centre).

The sheer scale of the project meant that it would take many years to complete, and although it had started in 1938 it was stalled following the surrender of Italy to the Allied Forces in 1941. The only market buildings to have been completed by that date were those at the east end of the square, both on the sides and in the centre (see page 128, centre right), and one section near the tribunal. The Eritrean grain market and tribunal occupied the centre of the square at its western end (top right). Some architects continued to adhere to Ferrazza's scheme after the Second World War and up to 1952, staying faithful to the original proposals (centre right). Since the 1950s, however, there has been little progress except for the relatively recent construction of sheltered market stalls now occupying the length of the square. As the major market and local bus station, the area remains at the centre of the life of the city.

GRAND MOSQUE

Original name Kulafa Al Rashidin Mosque
Current address Selam Street/Ad Ebrihim
Original address Via Piemonte/Largo Puglie
Architect unknown; Giuseppe Arata (1943)
Date 1906; redeveloped 1937–38, 1943
Map reference C11

In 1906 the first mosque was built in Asmara. It stood on raised ground just west of the Orthodox church, overlooking the eastern edge of the city and the hills of Gheza Banda to the south. For many years it was relatively isolated, though to the west many simple stone dwellings were erected around the market. By the 1930s, however, the open spaces in front of and behind the mosque were soon to be incorporated in the grand master plan for the city. About 1937 the old mosque was demolished and replaced by a larger 'Grand Mosque', accommodating the now burgeoning Muslim population of Asmara. As one major element in Guido Ferrazza's scheme, the Grand Mosque stood at the intersection of the market square and Ad Ebrihim. Curiously, conforming to this urban plan proved more of a priority than aligning the mosque with Mecca, as is usually the norm. The squares in front and behind would extend from the former Viale Milano in the north to the fountain of Mai Jah Jah at the foot of the hills of Gheza Banda in the south. The part of the square behind the mosque was called Largo Libya; that in front was Largo Puglie, which ran from the former Corso del Re to the former Viale Mussolini. However, the plan was never fully implemented, and the section of the square south of the former Viale Mussolini was abandoned and absorbed into the surrounding street plan and a small park. In the 1950s the municipality building was later constructed on the park. Largo Puglie remained intact, and contained the fish and vegetable markets designed by Ferrazza and built before the Grand Mosque (see page 129, bottom). The style of these buildings, with round-arched colonnades, is similar to that of the market, while the concrete and glass dome of the vegetable market is comparable to that of the Grand Mosque.

The fusion of Moorish and Roman stylistic elements in these buildings is interesting, and one might assume it was a result of Ferrazza's previous experience in Tripoli. The Grand Mosque, which has a fluted minaret and round-arched portico and colonnades on either side, is a distinctly Italianate version of the original mosque, which had a simple minaret, octagonal in plan, and horseshoe-arch doorway and windows. The interior of the Grand Mosque is dominated by a large central concrete and glass dome with fine painted decoration in an Islamic style (see page 133). Below the dome and throughout the interior is a series of simplified vaults supported on columns linked by Moorish lancet arches, decorated in a similar manner to the dome. In front of the Grand Mosque was built a large prayer square. In the centre, patterned in the cobbling, were three *fasces* and the letters "XVI", indicating the date of construction to be the year 16 in Mussolini's calendar, *i.e.* 1938. The cobbles marking the year have been removed, but the *fasces* remain.

In 1943, "under the request of the Muslim community of Asmara", the architect Giuseppe Arata was commissioned to incorporate into the mosque the pedestrian walkways that linked the former Largo Libya with the mosque square and the former Largo Puglie, thereby increasing its capacity (near right). This alteration effectively undermined the original plan to integrate these two vast squares, which were designed to traverse Asmara. Pedestrian access is now markedly restricted, which considerably diminishes the attractiveness and usefulness of the former Largo Puglie and Largo Libya as integrated urban spaces.

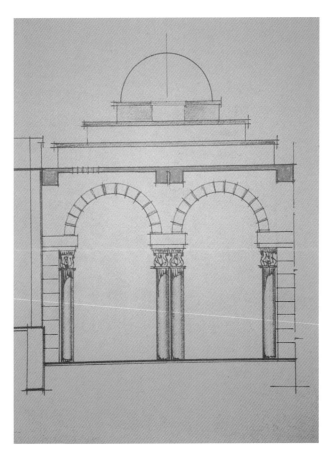

ENDA MARIAM ORTHODOX CATHEDRAL AND DEGGHI SELAM

Original name Biet Christian
Current address Arbate Asmara Street
Original address Arbate Asmara
Architect Enda Mariam: E. Gallo (1920); unknown (1938–39);
Degghi Selam: Odoardo Cavagnari
Date Enda Mariam: 1920, 1938–39; Degghi Selam: 1917
Map reference C12

The original village of Arbate Asmara was once located on the site now occupied by the Orthodox cathedral. However, after the Italians arrived, the village was moved to the north-east outskirts of the city. The original site remained of vital importance to the indigenous Eritrean Orthodox community, since their church stood on the crest of the hill where the present cathedral is located. The original church was a *hidmo*, constructed using the 'monkey-head' technique and topped with an Orthodox cross (above). It was surrounded by a wall and trees. The walls of the interior were decorated with brightly coloured paintings of saints, one of them even being of the tribal leader Ras Alula. Sacred scriptures in the ancient language of Ge'ez were also stored in the church.

Asmara's rapidly growing Orthodox population soon outgrew the modest Orthodox church, and so in 1920 an Italian architect, E. Gallo, designed a second church to replace the original. Like Cavagnari's Degghi Selam, the new church featured *agdo*-style roofs on the two towers that stood in front of the main church, at each corner (top right). These towers were used for storing religious objects and clothing. The main church was rectangular in plan and had a raised central nave, and its walls were built using the 'monkey-head' technique, with dowels of white juniper. Windows and doorways were set in stepped frames that provided ample shade and emphasized the building's overall solidity. It is evident that the architects of these buildings were respectful of local vernacular architecture.

A new church very similar in style to Gallo's earlier design, but more simplified in form and considerably larger, replaced the church of 1920 in 1938. The foundation stone was laid on 27 September 1938. Two massive towers stood at the entrance, with the main church building set behind and between them (bottom left). The towers, square in plan, retained *agdo* roofs, but these were separated from the layered stone by additional white concrete sections with vertical openings. Although dowels were not used, the layering of stone in horizontal banding imitated the style employed in traditional 'monkey-head' construction.

The main church building has a simple rectangular plan; the interior is decorated with a huge decorative and vibrantly coloured mosaic depicting religious figures. The composition is divided into seven sections, each one containing a single figure above which is a large Orthodox cross. Below the mosaic is the main entrance, composed of two round-arched doorways, on both sides of which are two small windows. As in Gallo's design, the doors and windows have stepped frames. A wall with a gateway, in a similar style to that of the church, now encloses the entire compound and almost completely blocks any view from outside of Cavagnari's Degghi Selam.

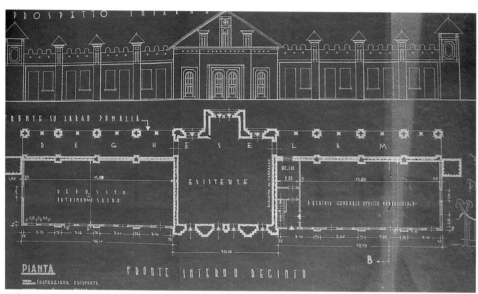

An outlying building, Degghi Selam, at the entrance of the church compound was designed in 1917 by the renowned engineer Odoardo Cavagnari. It incorporates many references to indigenous Eritrean architecture, in particular the conical concrete roofs of the *agdo*, placed at either end of the building and above its central portion. Below each roof are panels on which angels are painted in the Orthodox style. Concrete crossbeams protrude from the upper walls, imitating the 'monkey-head' technique, and wooden beams used in the building's construction were obtained from the old church compound.

SAN FRANCESCO CHURCH

Original name San Francesco Church
Current address Rahayta Street/Mereb Street, Gejeret
Original address Piazza San Francesco
Architect Paolo Reviglio
Date 1938
Map reference 16/17

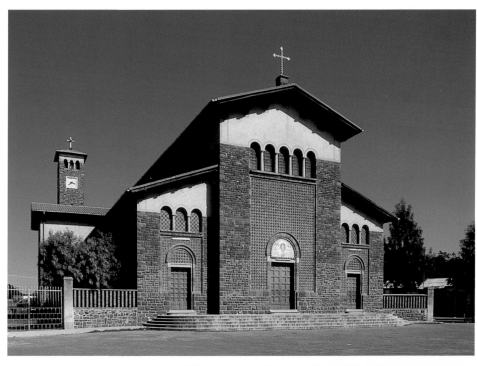

The foundation stone of this church, which was constructed under the supervision of the renowned engineer Paolo Reviglio, was laid on 21 April 1938; the church was completed and blessed on 24 November 1939. The rooms for the Capuchin Friars in the grounds were completed on 11 May 1940. The church is in a Romanesque style, with plain brickwork on the lower and centre portions of the façade, and plastered walls from the window arches to the roof. The main entrance is a rectangular doorway set in a large arched frame. Inside the church a wide nave flanked by broad aisles leads to a newly refurbished altar (the original was removed during the 1970s). The interior is lightly decorated, with the walls of the nave painted to give the illusion of galleries above. Behind the church, to the north-east, is a tall campanile with a clock and three round arches on each side. The Art Deco-style monument of St Francis of Assisi in the square in front of the church was erected in 1953.

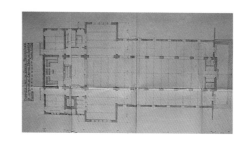

SAN ANTONIO CHURCH

Original name San Antonio Church
Current address Decemhare Road, Godaif
Original address Decemhare Road, Godaif
Architect Roberto Cappellano
Date 1940
Map reference (off the map)

This small church built for the village of Godaif, now an area on the southern outskirts of the city, has been designed in a simplified Romanesque style. Its façade, with three tall arches and mosaic decoration, is striking, not least because both Orthodox and Catholic images are depicted in the mosaics. These were modified under the Ethiopian Dergue régime by Padre Ruffino, a supporter of Eritrean independence, who used to conduct his services in Tigrinya and keep an Eritrean flag hidden in his church. The words *fede, speranze* and *carita* (faith, hope and charity) once appeared in the arches. A small bell-tower stands at the north-east corner of the church.

At the rear of the church is a small courtyard with colonnades of simple brick arches, similar to those at the front of the church and on the bell-tower. The nave is relatively small. One of the more interesting details inside the church is the large skylight at the east end, which allows bright sunlight to illuminate the altar naturally and effectively.

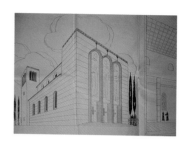

ASMARA SOAP FACTORY

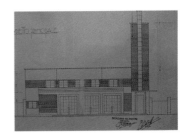

Original name Sedi del Reale Automobile Club d'Italia (RACI) (Head Offices of the Royal Automobile Club of Italy)
Current address Mai Bela Avenue/Arerib Street
Original address Viale 24 Maggio/Via P. Rolle
Architect Giuseppe Borziani
Date 1937
Map reference C5/C6

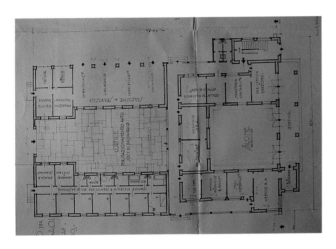

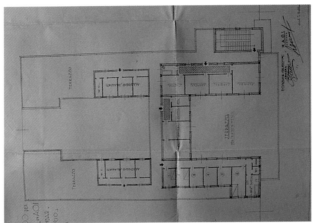

The drawings and plan for this building, approved in 1937, bear the label "Design for the head offices of the RACI in A.O.I. [Africa Orientale Italiana]: Addis Abeba, Gondar, Harar, Mogadiscio, Asmara". The building was designed to include a service station with an official checkpoint for the clients and their vehicles, a showroom, a sheltered courtyard for parking (10 metres [33 feet] wide) and a small hotel, on both ground and first floors, for visiting members of the club. The small turret was designed to contain the water tank. Situated on the first floor were the living quarters of the club's director, an Italian mechanic and of course the native employees. The director's living quarters opened on to a terrace for parties, which were no doubt enlivened by a gramophone and perhaps even

dancing, as was typical in the 1930s. The small size of the courtyard on the floor plan suggests that the first work of the morning for the employees was to push outside the dozen or so cars parked there in rows, since there was not enough space provided for cars to turn. The design is unquestionably influenced by Rationalism, though it is not fully adhered to. The departure from pure Rationalism can be observed in the perspective drawing (opposite, centre), which illustrates the doorway of the tower, the three main entrances and the windows with chamfered, not right-angled, frames.

The present building bears little resemblance to the original design described above, owing to the extensive modifications that have

taken place since its construction. The most obvious changes include the construction of a second floor projecting from the left of the turret, thereby obscuring the turret completely and destroying the original composition (opposite, bottom left). Additionally, the roof terrace has been integrated within the rest of the building, and so the once vacant space above the three windows has been filled in. The narrow concrete coping can still be seen projecting from the left and right wings below the second floor, giving a clue to the building's original form. Another alteration is the concrete wall that conceals most of the building from the street, although the top parts of the three entrances are still just visible above it.

Another very similar though less Rationalist-inspired building was constructed next to the RACI Head Office, with a larger and more dominant tower. The tower contains three rooms placed one above another, with windows facing the street, linked by an external metal stairway on the rear wall. It is assumed that the unusual arrangement of this staircase, allowing access to the ground floor of the building from the tower, was to allow the manager to check on his staff on his way out. The arched windows on the far left of this building are at variance with the Rationalist style of the tower, though it is unclear whether they are original or are later additions.

APARTMENTS

Original name Società Anonima Alfa Romeo (SAAR)
Current address 177-1 Street
Original address Viale Armando Diaz
Architect unknown
Date approximately 1937
Map reference G7/H7

Alfa Romeo was one of many Italian industrial firms to establish branch offices in Eritrea in the 1930s. This building once housed the company's head office in the colony; it administered a large number of garages and residential buildings for the company's workers. The central section of the building is raised slightly above the height of the two plainer wings. The most striking feature of the building is its immense entrance, which has a colossal chamfered frame constructed in plastered breeze blocks. The edges of the steps up to the entrance conform to the angle of the chamfer. The building's original decorative elements are intact: the name "Alfa Romeo" still hangs between two decorated flagpoles and the light fittings on either side of the entrance. The vertical and horizontal symmetry of the façade is emphasized by two levels of six rectangular windows, each with a narrow concrete frame. The angled cornice on the wings of the building pays clear reference to the shape of the frame of the entrance; the lack of a cornice on the central section also enhances the monumentality of that part of the building.

SILICON FACTORY

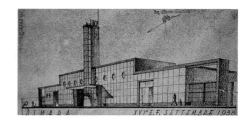

Original name Agenzia Lancia
Current address Tegadelti Street
Original address Godaif Road
Architect Carlo Marchi and Carlo Montalbetti
Date 1938
Map reference J5

One of the most striking industrial buildings in Asmara, this former complex housing a service station, workshops, showroom and car exchange for the Italian car company Lancia was built by a wealthy Italian, Salvatore Falletta, who is better known for building the Palazzo Falletta next to the cathedral (see pages 174–75). Certain Art Deco tendencies are arguably evident in the building, for example its bold symmetry (undermined by two additional porthole windows at the southern end of the building), stepped outline, porthole windows and projecting central tower housing a water tank.

Illuminated at night, the tower would have been a beacon for those returning to the city from the southern towns in the evening. A small office at the base of the tower was constructed in glass to conform to the rest of the tower. On either side of the office are entrances similar in design to those of the old City Sanitation Office (see page 126). It is interesting to note that the original design proposed only one concrete frame at either end of the building, when in fact three were constructed. The building remains in very good condition, though the wall now separating it from the street makes it almost impossible to appreciate the form of the building fully from outside the compound.

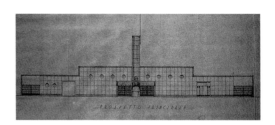

BRITISH AND AMERICAN TOBACCO
GROUP OFFICES

Original name Sede del Monopolio Tabacchi (Head Office of the Monopolio Tobacco Company)
Current address Felket Street
Original address Via Cavour
Architect unknown
Date approximately 1938
Map reference F10

This building, unusual in form, has remained the offices of one of Eritrea's tobacco suppliers since it was built in the late 1930s. The façade is composed of five main elements: a central entrance once ornamented with two large vertical *fasces*; an intermediary section on either side of the entrance, each with a single window on both floors; and two very distinctive projecting curved wings.

The façade was altered considerably during a relatively recent renovation – though the *fasces* on either side of the entrance were probably removed soon after the Italians were defeated in 1941. The poles on which the axe-heads hung are still evident. The windows on either side of the entrance have also been altered; an attempt to represent their original form by painting the area they originally occupied is largely unsuccessful because the new shutters, when open, disrupt the vertical lines. The building has a rounded architrave, and a simplified frieze and entablature, broken only by the projecting entrance. It is difficult to appreciate the restored building in its entirety, since its most distinctive features – the wings – are largely hidden behind palm trees.

SHELL SERVICE STATION

Original function AGIP service station
Current address Decemhare Road, Godaif
Original address Decemhare Road, Godaif
Architect unknown
Date 1937
Map reference (off the map)

On the southern outskirts of Asmara, this small service station was once the last place to fill cars with petrol before the southern Eritrean towns of Decemhare and Adi-Ugri. Designed in a distinctively nautical Moderne style, the building, along with many others in a similar style all over Eritrea, was commissioned by the Italian petrol company AGIP. Most of these service stations can still be seen today, the smallest of them merely round huts with just two porthole windows on either side. This example is one of the largest in Eritrea. With its curved form, porthole windows and brightly lit signage originally placed on the street (but now removed), this quirky building reflects the influence of international Modernist architecture from the 1920s and 1930s.

WORKSHOP AND SERVICE STATION

Original function Fiat Tagliero service station
Current address Mereb Street/Sematat Avenue
Original address Via Ugo di Fazio/Viale de Bono
Architect Giuseppe Pettazzi
Date 1938
Map reference H5

The design of this former Fiat service station, without question one of Asmara's most extraordinary buildings, clearly imitates the streamlined and dynamic form of an aeroplane. With such bold stylistic references that celebrate modern transport and travel, this building must be considered as one of Africa's finest examples of Futurist architecture. Interestingly, it is very similar in form to an earlier design for a service station by the American architect Frank Lloyd Wright (bottom left).

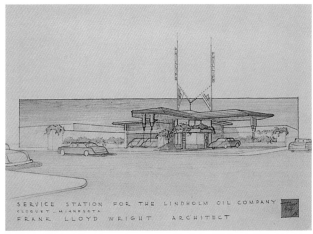

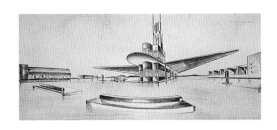

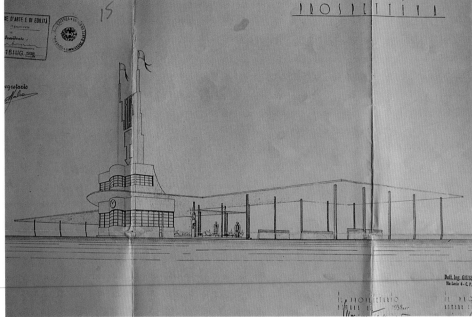

The structure itself was a remarkable feat of engineering for the time. With a thirty-metre (ninety-seven-foot) span, the cantilevered concrete wings hang literally unsupported above street level, providing ample shade for those working below. Since some members of the municipality had reservations about the structural integrity or mathematical viability of this building, the architect, Giuseppe Pettazzi, had to include pillars propping up the wings when formally submitting his designs for the building to be approved (above right). These pillars were in the form of wooden posts; on the inauguration of the building, in order to prove his calculations were correct, Pettazzi was allegedly forced to put a gun to the head of the hesitant builder who had been assigned the task of removing the pillars. With such forced persuasion, the builder knocked down the posts, and the cantilevered wings remained horizontal.

The central section of the building is composed of numerous visually striking stepped elements. Along with the tall flagpoles, the wrap-around windows on the ground and first floors, and the ample space for typographic advertising, not to mention the incredible cantilevered wings, these make the building a most interesting and eccentric structure.

STORE

Original function Spinelli store
Current address Saro Street
Original address unknown
Architect unknown
Date late 1930s
Map reference G9

This large general storage facility was commissioned by the Italian businessman Spinelli, who was presumably the owner of the nearby Villa Spinelli (see pages 118–19). The distinctive circular walls of the compound, the enormous concrete framework of the two entrances, and the brick frame surrounding the central part of the building with the doorway leading to the offices inside, provide an imposing frontage.

The colossal walls are constructed of layered stone and brick in a manner similar to those of Enda Mariam Orthodox Cathedral and many industrial buildings of this era. The technique is designed to provide extra stability and strength, in the same way that traditional Eritrean construction methods employed layers of stone between horizontal bands of wood. The walls, rather than simply enclosing the compound, are the exterior walls of deep rooms and storage spaces. Inside the compound a separate circular building is positioned in the centre of the circular courtyard, a road around which provides access to all the storage areas.

MINISTRY OF TOURISM

Original function Lloyds building
Current address Harnet Avenue/Mata Street
Original address Viale Mussolini/Via Dalmazia
Architect unknown
Date approximately 1938
Map reference D10

This building features an interesting arrangement of a series of small glass panes wrapped around a curved corner, on either side of which (to the south and east) are imposing concrete structures. The simplicity of the concrete structures (containing eighteen rooms) is evocative of many Rationalist buildings, although the curved corner is not true to that style. At ground level the shop entrances are simple rectangular openings with narrow marble frames, while the upper floors house offices with French windows opening on to individual shaded balconies. Access to the offices is provided by a single entrance at street level. The building extends beyond the concrete framework, with another nine windows facing Harnet Avenue and three on the eastern façade. This building probably predates the one in a similar style adjoining it to the west, since it appears in the proposals for that building of 1939 (see page 184). The date for the construction of this building is, therefore, probably 1938.

APARTMENT BUILDING

Original name Adriano Cave
Current address Maryam Gmbi Street
Original address Via Oriani
Architect Antonio Rovelli
Date 1938; extended 1939
Map reference G5

Several buildings were originally proposed for this site, including an office and apartment complex as well as a cinema. The apartment building that received planning permission was constructed in 1938 but was extended a year later to incorporate buildings to the south. The design of the finished building is a rather peculiar mixture of styles, with some Rationalist-inspired elements such as the balconies and windows, but overall there appears to be more of a Romanesque influence, as indicated by the use of arches and semicylindrical roof tiles.

However, the original building was more overtly Romanesque than it is today, once incorporating three large arches at the front entrance and other smaller arches elsewhere on the building, including three on the rear of the parapet. The three arches at the entrance have since been filled in. The original design also shows some artistic licence in its depiction of gladiatorial figures, camels, lions, coconut palms and onlookers sporting fezzes; this suggests that the architect, who was based in Genoa, might not have visited Eritrea. The design, with so many Romanesque references, is perhaps more synonymous with buildings found in Tripoli than with those of the Eritrean highlands.

SELAM HOTEL

Original name Albergo CIAAO (Compagnia Immobiliare Alberghi Africa Orientale)
Current address Maryam Gmbi Street
Original address Via Oriani
Architect Rinaldo Borgnino
Date 1937
Map reference D6/E6

Designed in Rome for an Italian hotel chain in East Africa, the Selam Hotel is perhaps Asmara's purest example of Rationalist architecture, as evidenced by its uncomplicated form and the geometric simplicity of its elements. For some unknown reason the design of the finished building reverses that shown on the original proposal, with the four square windows on the ground floor placed south of the entrance, and the veranda, which disrupts the symmetry of the façade, to the north. Apart from the mirroring of the floor plan, perhaps the most striking difference between the proposed and actual designs is the closed veranda. It is unclear whether this was closed off at the time of construction or later, since old photographs show it incorporated into the dining area, as it remains today. The entrance is contained within a porch projecting from the façade. In the proposal there are no windows on either side of the entrance; they were added later and do little to enhance the original geometrical composition. The *fasces* – symbol of the Fascist regime – adorned the spaces where the windows are now positioned.

The ground floor contains the dining-room and restaurant, kitchen, bar, reception, offices and a series of four guest rooms, each with en-suite bathroom and lavatory. The overall plan is square, with a central courtyard, and service quarters at the rear. The 'L'-shaped first floor contains more guest rooms, some with en-suite and others with shared bathroom facilities. The uniformity of the upper-floor windows along the front is the result of the regular arrangement of double rooms without a bathroom, while the smaller evenly spaced windows along the side walls serve the rooms with en-suite bathrooms, each room and bathroom having a single window. The front windows are actually doorways giving access to individual recessed balconies that provide ample shade. The interior fixtures and fittings remain largely unchanged since the 1930s, making the building perhaps one of Asmara's most original interiors. Fortunately, plans to increase the height of the building to three floors after independence were shelved. The Selam Hotel might also be regarded as one of Eritrea's most historically significant buildings, since it was here on 27 April 1993 that the head of the United Nations Observer Mission in Eritrea, Mr Semir Sambar, declared Eritrea an independent state following the almost unanimous result of a referendum.

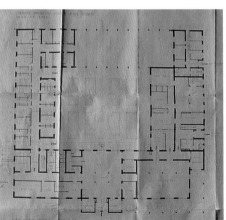

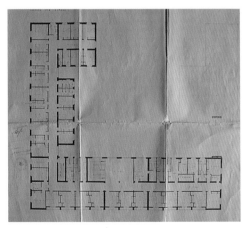

MINISTRY OF LAND, WATER AND THE ENVIRONMENT

Original function casino
Current address 194-2 Street
Original address Via Lunigiana
Architect unknown
Date late 1930s
Map reference E11

Known infamously in the past as the home of Asmara's most exclusive brothel for Italian officers, this rather unusual building, also incorporating a casino and bar, was built around the end of the 1930s. Its site, south-east of Harnet Avenue, was among the last in the city centre to be developed. The symmetry of the building is apparent on all of its four exterior walls but is most evident on the façade, where it is underlined by the use of distinctive decorative columns of indented horizontal banding that contrast with the verticality of the terrace above the entrance. Apart from this banding the walls on either side of the entrance are left plain; the side walls, which are not visible when the building is viewed from the front, have horizontal windows in a vertical strip. There is a definite visual emphasis on the entrance and the terrace, as both project slightly from the central part of the building. The creation of the terrace as part of the first floor, rather than as a separate space on the roof, is a very interesting architectural solution that accentuates the composition of the different elements around the entrance. The building's other exterior walls remain relatively plain, with a symmetrical arrangement of windows and doorways disrupted only by the modern downpipes.

PRINTING PRESS

Original name Cinema Hamasien
Current address Aayget Street
Original address Via Degias Tesfamariam
Architect Inginio Marebelli
Date 1936
Map reference A12

Situated in the old native quarter, the Cinema Hamasien was the first purpose-built cinema, and therefore the first means of entertainment on a large scale, for the Eritrean population. Seating for up to 760 people is arranged in two tiers; most of the seats are in the stalls downstairs and the rest are in the gallery. The cinema occupies the top two floors of the building, while a printing press is now located on the ground floor. The cinema is in urgent need of restoration, though the original projector still remains in its box at the rear of the building.

Certain alterations to the building have unbalanced its original proportions. The most obvious is the filling-in of the space in the south-east corner of the building on the main road, in which are set small square windows. These conflict visually with the arches used for openings throughout the rest of the building and decoratively on the cornice on the north-east corner. Access to the building is from the street or from the staircase adjoining the southern wall that leads to an arched doorway into the main reception.

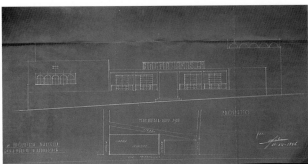

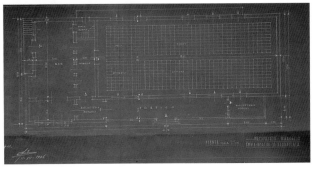

CINEMA ROMA

Original name Cinema Dux
Current address Sematat Avenue/171-4 Street
Original address Viale de Bono/Via Ruspoli
Architect Roberto Cappellano (1937); Bruno Sclafani (1944)
Date original proposal 1937; second proposal 1944
Map reference F7

Strangely, the original proposal for this cinema, in 1937, was initially refused approval on the grounds that its name was too overt a reference to Il Duce (Mussolini). Construction appears to have taken place soon after 1937, and an early title for the cinema was Cinema Excelsior. The name Roma appears to have been adopted slightly later. The exterior features four entrances with double doors raised above street level by steps and set below a slender canopy on which ROMA, fabricated in metal, used to stand. Now the name appears on the marble-faced façade in large lettering below four square windows. Surrounding the marble facing is stucco decorated with a pattern of squares and painted to match the colour of the rest of the building. The seating inside the cinema is arranged in stalls, with an upper gallery situated above the lobby area that contains a bar and ticket booths. The cinema has been recently restored and the interior completely overhauled, with new seating, lobby, lighting, screen and sound system, making it Asmara's principal cinema. The recent restoration has used a rich range of reds, ochre and oranges for the interior and exterior decoration.

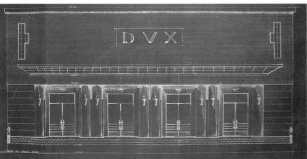

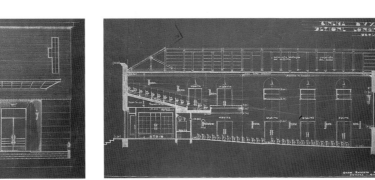

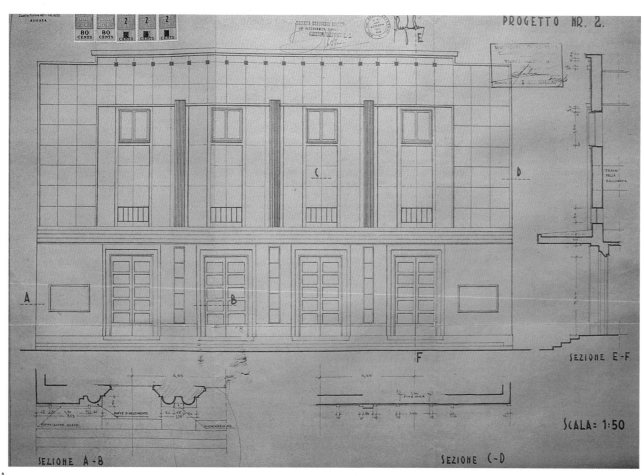

PROGETTO NR. 2.

SEZIONE E-F

SCALA= 1:50

SEZIONE A-B

SEZIONE C-D

CINEMA IMPERO

Original name Cinema Impero
Current address Harnet Avenue/176-21 Street
Original address Viale Mussolini/Via Lorenzini
Architect Mario Messina
Date 1937
Map reference D10/D11

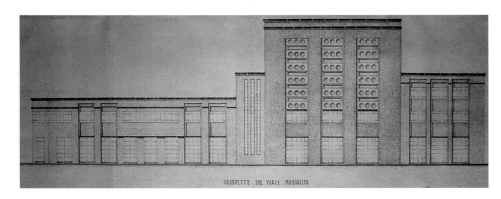

PROSPETTO SUL VIALE MUSSOLINI

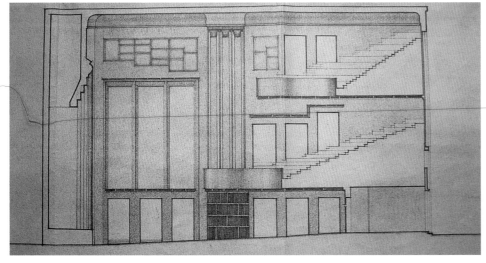

The original design for the Cinema Impero complex was an ambitious proposal that included a three-storey cinema seating 1800 people, a billiard hall, a restaurant, a café, a bar, shops, apartments and offices. Occupying an entire block, it would have had entrances on the east and south. However, the actual building was more modest, probably owing to financial constraints, though still easily one of Asmara's largest developments in the late 1930s. It incorporated a two-storey cinema, bars and shops at ground level, and offices on the three upper floors. The provision of access to the cinema from the east was also abandoned.

The façade of the cinema on Harnet Avenue remains one of the most distinctive in Asmara and is an exceptional example of 1930s cinema design. It features three white columns containing strip windows separated by rows of circular lights, framed by the vertical arrangement of the letters spelling out the name CINEMA IMPERO. The maroon colour of the façade complements these decorative elements, and the round lights and backlit lettering greatly enhance the appearance of the façade at night. At street level five doors provide access to the lobby, which retains some of its original fittings (see page 165, top); white marble staircases provide access to the gallery, and grey marble flooring is used elsewhere. Inside the auditorium, rows of wooden seats are set on a gently raked floor, and a row of decorative pillars topped with lions' heads separates the massive screen from the seating area (see page 165). The walls are adorned with interesting decorative stucco motifs of African imagery – dancers, palm trees and antelopes – in a vaguely Art Deco style.

164

ODEON CINEMA

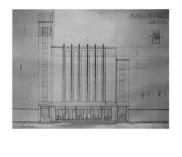

Original name Cinema O.D.E.O.N.
Current address Bihat Street
Original address Via G. Sapeto
Architect Giuseppe Zacche and Giuseppe Borziani
Date 1937
Map reference E8

Tucked away off Sematat Avenue, the Odeon Cinema is another fine example of cinema architecture from the 1930s. Though, like Cinema Impero, it is not as large as originally proposed, it is nonetheless an impressive structure. Influenced by the Novecento style, the façade is dominated by simplified vertical forms, in particular three strip windows set in slightly recessed frames. On either side of the main façade are two narrow wings with windows identical to the three in the central section of the building. The original design incorporated a high tower on the north-west corner of the façade, disrupting the symmetry of the building, though this was never constructed. Additionally, six vertical concrete strips separating five slender windows, stretching almost the entire height of the façade, would have dominated the central section.

Below the canopy seven doorways lead to the bar and lobby, though only the central one is now used. The bar on the south wall of the lobby is one of Asmara's finest historic interiors, designed in an Art Deco style characterized by vertical and horizontal lines, and enhanced with backlighting. The two spherical ceiling lights made of glass 'petals' are also notable. The auditorium, containing stalls and a gallery, is in need of restoration. Above the proscenium arch hangs an interesting plaster mask of a bearded man.

CAPITOL CINEMA

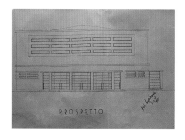

Original name Cinema Augustus
Current address Denden Street
Original address Viale Crispi
Architect Ruppert Saviele
Date 1938; destroyed by fire 1941; repaired 1944
Map reference D7

Built in 1938 for the Compagnia Immobiliare Alberghi Africa Orientale (CIAAO), an Italian hotel company in East Africa, this cinema is one of Asmara's more distinctive structures. Its style is often (probably mistakenly) described as Expressionist, perhaps owing to the rounded form of the front corners of the building, which correspond to the internal division of spaces and are emphasized by the diversity of different openings. These include narrow horizontal windows on the rounded corners and the large area at the front serving as the entrance to and exit from the building. The façade facing Denden Street has not been altered since it was repaired in 1944 after a fire caused extensive damage to the interior.

The interior includes a well-proportioned atrium, the low ceiling of which is supported by simple concrete pillars in order to maximize the available space within this confined area. The rooms adjoining the atrium include a bar, occupying one rounded corner in the front of the building (though accessed through a separate door on the far right), and an office, in the other corner. A separate entrance leads to private seating upstairs for dignitaries. The very large auditorium is simply fitted out, with light decorative detailing in the form of naked human figures in stucco. The cinema is the largest in Asmara, with seating for 1800 and a retractable roof for improved ventilation. The building is in urgent need of repair, and fortunately plans are currently under way to restore this magnificent building to its former glory.

POST OFFICE SQUARE (PROPOSED DESIGN)

Original name Piazza Roma
Current address Post Office Square
Original address Piazza Roma
Architect Studio Cappellano
Date 1937
Map reference D9

The former Piazza Roma can certainly be regarded as the historic commercial centre of Asmara. The area surrounded by the central post office, the former Bank of Rome and the shops along Nakfa Avenue and other streets was once an undeveloped area of urban land used for public gatherings. Before the mid-1930s it was transformed into a public park with a circular fountain at its centre. In 1937 a proposal to modernize this area through the construction of an underground centre was submitted to the municipality.

The overall design of the centre was Rationalist in style, with a rectangular plan and access at each corner. Telephones and secretarial services occupied the central area, with a bar at one end and men's and women's hairdressers at the other. Along each side of the complex ran cubicles for both women – each including a lavatory, sink and bath – and men – each with just a lavatory and sink; communal urinals were also provided for the men. A café and park were planned at street level. Ventilation was provided by an elaborate system drawing up air from the underground rooms to the street by a series of horizontal openings on the wall of the complex protruding above ground level. These can be seen facing the street in the perspective drawing (opposite, bottom).

The design for this elaborate complex was never executed, and the square remained largely redundant, eventually being filled up with car-parking space, which is how it remains. Returning this historic centre to use as a public park would perhaps do much to enhance such an important civic space.

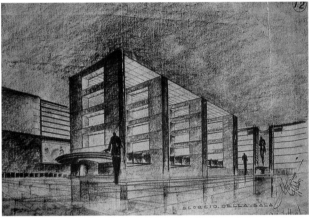

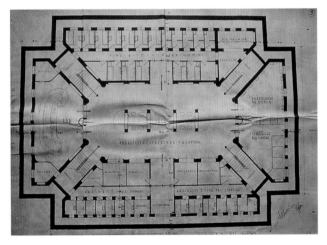

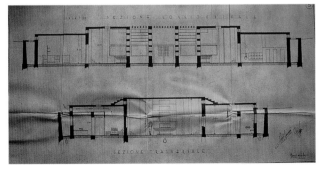

171

MAI JAH JAH

Original name La Fontana
Current address Marsa Teklay Street/173-18 Street
Original address Viale delle M. Doro/Viale M. Buonarroti
Architect unknown
Date 1938
Map reference F11

Although it features in early urban plans for Asmara, this fountain was not built until the late 1930s, when the suburb of Gheza Banda was laid out. The photograph here (left) shows the year of construction in Mussolini's calendar, XVI, corresponding to 1938, and the three *fasces* motifs, all of which have since been removed. The fountain was originally intended to form part of a grand civic development that included the market and mosque squares, and Mai Bela, but the proposals to incorporate the area between it and Harnet Avenue into the general gridded street plan took precedence. Although the fountain once backed on to the railway line that traversed the south-east districts of the city, it and the surrounding parks remain largely isolated, though they provide a very pleasant environment linking the city centre with the suburb of Gheza Banda.

The fountain is set in a residential area, with a circular access road on a gentle slope surrounding it. Within the boundary of the road are semicircular flowerbeds, separated from the fountain by two flights of steps on either side. The fountain itself consists of a series of four long steps, each of which has semicircular ends and is composed of four horizontal concrete bands. Surrounding each step is a rectangular trough feeding water to that below. The last trough on the lower tier, from which the water is pumped back up to the top of the fountain, is also semicircular in form. Fascist motifs once decorated each post on the lower street level, but they have since been removed and the posts plastered.

FALLETTA BUILDING

Original name Palazzo Falletta
Current address Harnet Avenue/Adi Hawesha Street/176-5 Street/176-7 Street
Original address Viale Mussolini/Via Regina/Via Prato/Via Bianchini
Architect Giuseppe Cane (1937); Carlo Marchi (1937–38); Aldo Burzagli (1938); A. Fulgini (1961)
Date 1937–38; renovated 1961
Map reference D9

The former Palazzo Falletta, designed for the prominent Italian businessman Salvatore Falletta, occupies a key site between the Catholic cathedral and the large commercial buildings on the west end of Harnet Avenue, and is one of the most important buildings on that street. The original design proposed only four storeys (top right), incorporating a tower at each corner, but it is now one of the few buildings in Asmara that was eventually taller than planned, with five floors. The form of the building is a modern adaptation of the medieval castle with corner towers. A similar design was used by the Italians for one of the government buildings in the western lowland town of Agordat. The striking chequered pattern is influenced by Novecento styling. Simple window frames finished in white plaster, and recessed balconies on each of the four sides linking the corner towers, provide an attractive contrast to the light-brown frame encasing them. At ground level the shop fronts have grey marble frames with chamfered corners.

The plan is a slightly distorted square, with a central courtyard in which stands a fine stone urn. The towers in each corner contain the stairwells, which were adapted to include lifts in 1961, when the building was renovated. Each stairwell provides access to three apartments on each floor, with a total of twelve apartments on each level. The renovation scheme of 1961 involved the conversion of some of these flats into office space, requiring sections of the interior corridor to be opened up. An entrance to the courtyard at ground level on the east side, proposed as part of the renovations, was not constructed.

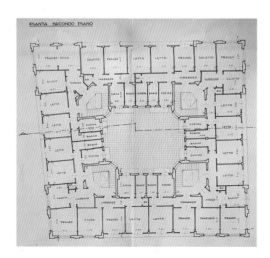

SHOPS AND APARTMENTS

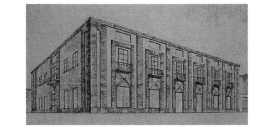

Original function shops and apartments
Current address Nakfa Avenue/176-21 Street
Original address Corso del Re/Via Lorenzini
Architect Domenico Rapisardi
Date 1937
Map reference D11

This office and apartment building is designed in a Novecento style. Six series of windows are separated vertically by various plaster mouldings, surrounding each set of windows above the individual balconies. The vertical alignment of these various components is accentuated by the different colours in which they have been painted: the background is white, each window space yellow and the moulded plaster strip framing it red. Separating the two upper floors is a simple rectangular plaster panel painted white.

Below each balcony is positioned a doorway for each shop at street level. A simplified plaster entablature completes the composition at the top of the building. The sides of the building are not as elaborate as the façade, though the rear is similar but without balconies. A number of large developments were proposed for Nakfa Avenue in the late 1930s; this building remains as one of just a few that were actually built.

SHOPS AND APARTMENTS

Original name Palazzo Minneci
Current address 176-1 Street/Segali Street
Original address Piazza della Posta
Architect Francesco Botteri of Studio Carlo Marchi
Date 1939
Map reference D9

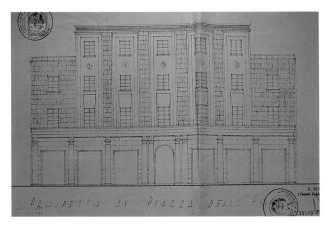

This distinctive building, designed for Vittorio Minneci (his second on this site) and dominating the western side of the small square in front of the central post office, was once said to be one of the finest examples of a privately funded apartment building in Asmara. Its façade is characterized by an eclectic mix of styles, with those used on the ground floor different from those on the upper floors. On the ground floor a series of trabeated Greek Doric columns supports a balcony that stretches the length of the first floor. However, an entrance composed of a Roman arch flanked by two columns breaks with the Greek styling (see page 178). One of the apartments in this building was once rented by an Israeli fugitive, Rahamim Mizrahi, who escaped from his British captors during the 1940s. He used this flat as a safe house for his compatriots who were also actively involved in the Israeli independence movement at that time.

Above are three floors of apartments designed in a distinctly Novecento style, with terraces occupying each corner of the roof. Strong vertical emphasis is achieved through the plaster mouldings and surface finishes framing the windows in five distinct bands. The doorways of the shops on the ground floor are aligned with these windows. The building, which has an 'H'-shaped plan, extends to the street behind (Segali Street). The façade here is a simplified version of the main façade but without the Greek-style colonnade at ground level. A narrow stairwell gives access to four apartments on each floor, while an inner courtyard separates both blocks of the building. An earlier design for a smaller version of this building was submitted for approval but clearly never used (see page 177, top right), though some of its features, including the references to Greek architecture on the ground floor and the vertical alignment of the upper-floor windows, were retained in what was actually built.

SHOPS AND APARTMENTS

Original name Palazzo Lazzarini
Current address Nakfa Avenue/Segeneyti Street
Original address Corso del Re/Mai Bela
Architect Roberto Cappellano
Date 1937
Map reference D10

After the course of the Mai Bela River was covered over in 1936, it was transformed into a road with buildings on either side. This Rationalist-style building occupying the centre of the street, where it joins Nakfa Avenue, was planned in 1937. The rather unusual shape of the site required the buildings to be not just long and narrow in form but also curved, to follow the course of the riverbed.

The façade on Nakfa Avenue is one of the most prominent features of this series of buildings, and a number of similar proposals for it were submitted. The restricted site meant that the architect created a design that minimized the use of space at street level, while providing additional space on the first and second floors through the use of overhanging balconies and rooms, which also give some shelter at street level.

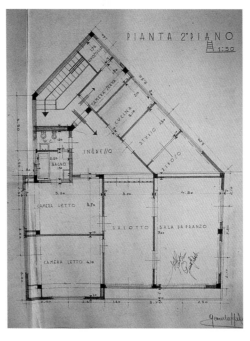

The final design is perhaps not as stylized as the concept drawing (right), with its wrap-around windows, although its windows and doorways are aligned vertically, as is shown in an alternative design above. The recessed ground floor of the building looks as if it has been 'carved' from the solid block above, which makes the building appear slightly top-heavy. Given the confined site on which the building is situated, this design solution is perhaps a reasonable compromise.

SHOPS AND APARTMENTS

Original function shops and apartments
Current address Harnet Avenue
Original address Viale Mussolini
Architect unknown
Date 1937
Map reference D10

Positioned among the three- and four-storey buildings opposite the cathedral, this somewhat monumental building was one of the first large structures along the former Viale Mussolini. It was, no doubt, once a colourful addition to this row of early shop and apartment buildings: its distinctive central stairwell has faded red paintwork, and the two wings are a faded yellow. This building, now in need of restoration, would have once been at the very heart of Italian Asmara; the perspective concept drawing depicts sleek cars and well-dressed Italians in fur coats.

The proportions of the building are not as consistent as those of others in Asmara: the ground-floor shop fronts are not consistent with the windows on the first and second floors. The central column containing the stairwell, which is marked by a vertical window above the entrance, extends upwards to a flagpole that provides the crowning detail to the building. The verticality of the central column is emphasized by the slender lines running up its sides and the division of the stairwell window into vertical rectangular sections. At the base of the central column is the entrance, enclosed by a bold and heavy grey marble frame with chamfered corners and surrounded by slender lines to accentuate the impression of solidity.

SHOPS AND APARTMENTS

Original name Palazzo Gheresadik
Current address Nakfa Avenue/Ad Ebrihim
Original address Corso del Re/Largo Puglie
Architect Carlo Marchi
Date 1938
Map reference D11

On the corner of Nakfa Avenue and the square in front of the Grand Mosque, this commercial development was designed to complement the surrounding buildings, which include the fish and vegetable markets designed by Ferrazza, the Grand Mosque itself, and the other buildings in front of the mosque. The common characteristic of these buildings is the use of the arch; here it is employed purely decoratively, in a similar manner to the low relief arches surrounding the doorways and windows on the façades of existing and earlier proposed buildings adjacent to the mosque. In nearby market buildings and on the Grand Mosque the main use of the arch is in colonnades and on the portico. The convex corner on the upper two floors, punctured only by porthole windows, is a curious detail, though it does serve to provide additional space for the view of the square and the Grand Mosque.

SHOPS AND APARTMENTS

Original name Palazzo Mazzetti
Current address Harnet Avenue/Denkel Street
Original address Viale Mussolini/Via Istria
Architect Aldo Burzagli
Date 1939
Map reference D10

One of the later structures built on Harnet Avenue before the end of the Italian régime, this Rationalist building dominates the open area where Mai Bela connects with Harnet Avenue. Its characteristic projecting concrete frame is sensitive to its neighbour, which employs a similar style. The frame provides considerable extra space for each apartment above ground level, while shading the street below. (It is uncertain why the actual structure has some windows without balconies, as they are shown with them in the proposed design: top right.) At the corner of the building the projecting frame is formed into wrap-around balconies offering superb unrestricted views of the cathedral and the western areas of the city for those apartments. All doorways and windows are aligned vertically and horizontally on the façade and sides of the building.

BAR ZILLI

Original function shops and apartments
Current address Sematat Avenue/Beirut Street
Original address Viale de Bono/Viale Nino Bixio
Architect unknown
Date late 1930s
Map reference F6

Constructed some time in the late 1930s, this conspicuously modern building, which is unlike any other in Asmara, faces north, overlooking the first major crossroads on the road to Decemhare leading out of the city centre. Several similar buildings were proposed for this roundabout, but none had such a mixture of details and styles as this one. It is difficult to classify such an eclectic building, since its peculiar individual features tend to obscure its overall form. The rows of porthole windows between the ground and second floors and the curved façade with its central vertical window and narrow horizontal strips in the bottom corners are separated awkwardly by rounded marble banding. The building has shops on the ground floor and apartments on the upper floors. A road used to pass behind the building until the Nyala Hotel was built on it in 1965.

SHOPS AND APARTMENTS

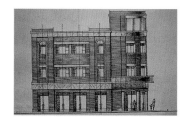

Original name Palazzo Berta
Current address 175-11 Street/Nakfa Avenue
Original address Via Martini/Corso del Re
Architect Antonio Vitaliti
Date 1939
Map reference D8

A fine example of Novecento architecture in Asmara, this building occupies a corner at the foot of the slope on which one of the city's most historic streets is situated. The finished building matches the original design clearly: the rounded corner is four storeys high, but the rest of the building behind it has only three levels. The increased height of the corner makes the building more prominent in relation to its location.

The sides of the building are unmistakably Novecento in style. On the side facing 175-11 Street, decorative arches top the columns in which the narrow windows are set. Between these two vertical components are the first- and second-floor windows, linked visually by white-painted lintels and protruding sills that are aligned horizontally with the lintels and sills of the narrow windows on either side. Vertical alignment is accentuated by the plain pilasters partitioning the façade, and by the columns on the main entrance on the ground floor and at the windows on the third floor. This emphasis on horizontal and vertical alignment is visible on all parts of the façade.

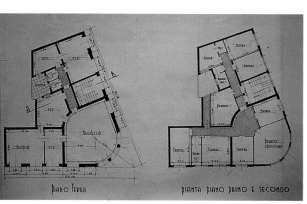

SHOPS AND APARTMENTS

Original name Sede del Gruppo Rion. Fascista
(Fascist District Group Head Office)
Current address Segeneyti Street
Original address Mai Bela
Architect Aldo Burzagli
Date 1939
Map reference C9/D9

Designed in 1939 to house the head office of the district group of the Fascist Party, this building was also intended to contain shops, apartments, offices and a garage. A classic example of overtly Fascist styling, intended to appeal to the future occupants of the building, is clearly shown in the proposed design (top right), which contrasts strongly with the diminutive and largely unimpressive form of the building itself. The gradient, curved course and narrow width of the road on which it is built do not perhaps make this a suitable location for a building with such supposed prestige, since its full impact cannot be appreciated.

The long two-storey structure sits awkwardly on its site; it has a rounded south corner leading into a façade on which upper-floor windows are aligned with the lower-floor doorways. The bold and rather crude entrance with a simple concrete frame, halfway along the façade, acts as the focal point of the building, but the length of the building and the curvature of its frontage make it hard to view either the entrance or the building in its entirety. Two staircases in the lobby, facing away from the doorway, provide access to the upper floor. The building is now much in need of restoration.

OFFICES AND BAR

Original name Palazzo Bahobesci
Current address Segeneyti Street
Original address Viale Badoglio
Architect Giuseppe Arata
Date 1936
Map reference C9

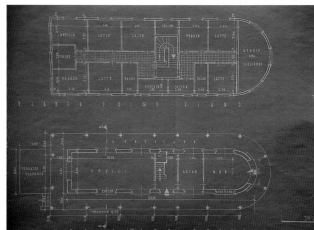

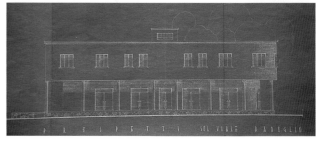

Designed for the renowned businessman Ahmed Ubed Bahobesci, this was the first modern building on the course of the Mai Bela River. Its distinctive form befits this unique location on the former river between the two winding roads leading from Nakfa Avenue to the north of the city. The colonnaded walkway around the ground floor provides pedestrian access around the building while maximizing office space on the upper floor. Vague stylistic references to various forms of transportation, particularly nautical, such as the semicircular form of the south end and the covered promenade, might be considered appropriate since the building stands not only between two roads but also on the course of a river. The building in the centre of the road and facing this one (see page 49, centre) might also be considered to draw references from certain modes of transport, such as a locomotive, and was built several years afterwards.

APARTMENT BUILDING

Original function apartment building
Current address Denden Street/Maryam Gmbi Street
Original address Viale Crispi/Via Oriani
Architect Aldo d'Alesio and Carlo Marchi
Date 1938
Map reference D5

Occupying the south-west corner of the junction between Denden Street and Maryam Gmbi Street, this apartment building, with a floor-plan in the shape of a quarter circle, is an attractive and simple solution to the problem of building on the corner of a major crossroads. Its three floors of apartments, each with a balcony and access to the street, are a carefully planned, almost Rationalist, design.

Inside, staircases on either side of the entrance lead to two apartments. Though the apartment on either side of the entrance occupies most of the front of the building, those at the rear have access to the balconies farthest from the entrance, as well as windows into the inner courtyard. The roof terrace has clearly been under-utilized and, like the apartments, is in need of restoration.

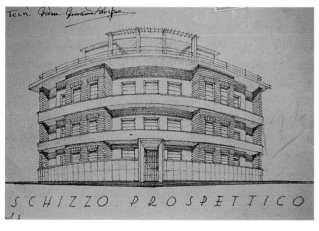

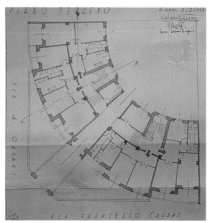

APARTMENTS

Original function apartments
Current address Bdho Avenue/Sematat Avenue
Original address Via Giuseppe Garibaldi/Viale de Bono
Architect unknown
Date unknown
Map reference F9 and F7

Relatively high-density, low-cost housing, of which these two apartment blocks are among the best examples in Asmara, is characteristic of the work of Guido Ferrazza, who had much experience and interest in this type of design. There is no proof, however, that he designed these two buildings. What is almost certain is that the same architect designed both, since they are almost identical and would have been built at the end of the 1930s to accommodate some of the many families arriving in Asmara at that time. The two prominent stairwells with their characteristic vertical windows provide access to the apartments. The arrangement of the apartments is similar on each floor, with four being served by each stairwell.

APARTMENTS

Original function apartments
Current address Munich Street/Awget Street
Original address Via Cossu
Architect Vincenzo di Giovine
Date 1939
Map reference C6

Like so many designs of the 1930s, the perspective drawing for this building depicts an austere Rationalist structure, which, though quite accurate, provides a distinctly different ambience from the actual building. Containing four two-bedroom apartments on each floor, the building has an attractive internal courtyard accessed through a central stairwell, the position of which is clearly marked by the imposing horizontal banding on the main façade. Having been extensively subdivided and altered, the building bears little resemblance to its original design, though some characteristics of the Rationalist style remain, in particular the horizontal windows of the stairwell. The suburb in which these apartments were built was the site of the sports stadium and horse-racing track until the late 1930s, so many of the plots have not been fully utilized. This building was an obvious attempt at providing high-density housing on a small scale.

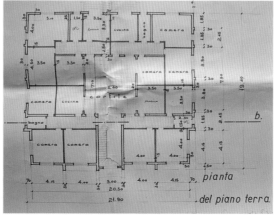

APARTMENTS

Original function maisonettes
Current address Koken Street/Golj Street
Original address Via Bandaccio/Via Colombo
Architect Carlo Pozzo
Date 1937
Map reference H4

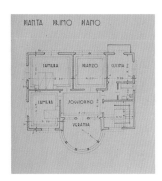

Near the former district of Campo Polo, these two buildings were designed by the architect Carlo Pozzo, who produced designs for many small villas around this time. The suburbs of Gaggiret, Godaif and Campo Polo were particularly suitable for such housing during the late 1930s and early 1940s, since the large areas of open land enabled immigrant Italians to build small dwellings with sufficient garden space there.

These two buildings appear to be relatively typical examples of the small villas constructed in these outer suburbs at this time, but their external appearance is deceptive as each houses two small two-bedroom apartments. In the first example (above), access to the ground-floor apartment is gained through the doorway at the front, while, unusually, the upper floor is reached by means of an external staircase on the right of the building that leads into an internal staircase

set in the front right corner of the building. Both apartments have identical floor-plans. The flats have been altered, and their verandas are now incorporated into the living areas. The second *villetta* (opposite) is designed on exactly the same principle, with access to the ground floor provided from the front and that to the first floor from the side. Here the first-floor apartment also has access to two balconies.

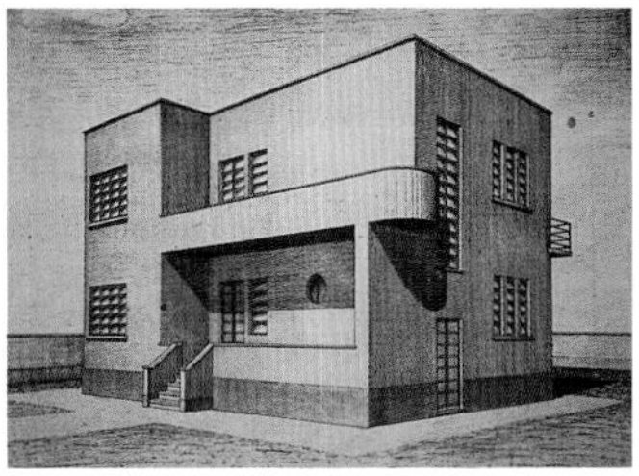

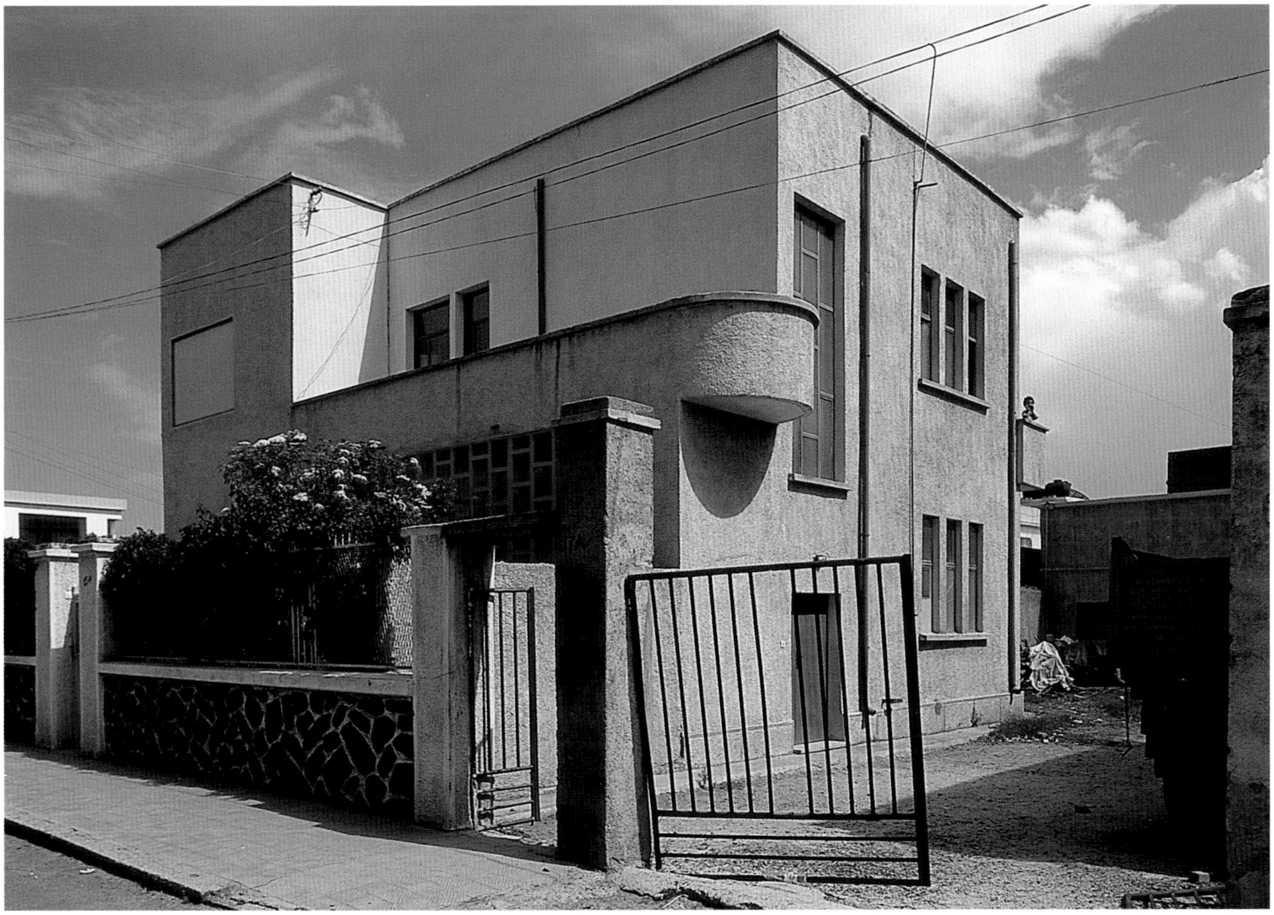

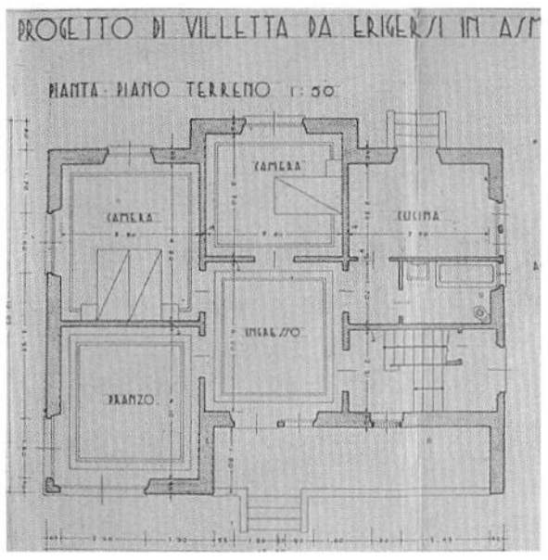
PROGETTO DI VILLETTA DA ERIGERSI IN AS
PIANTA PIANO TERRENO 1:50
CAMERA
CAMERA
CUCINA
INGRESSO
PRANZO

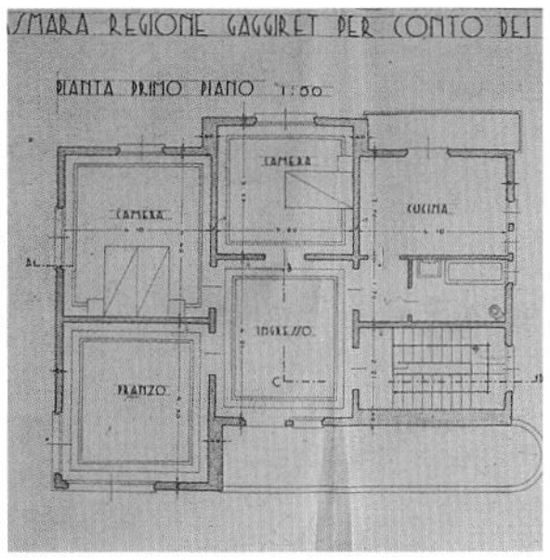
SMARA REGIONE GAGGIRET PER CONTO DEI
PIANTA PRIMO PIANO 1:50
CAMERA
CAMERA
CUCINA
INGRESSO
PRANZO

VILLAS

Original function villas
Current address Maryam Gmbi Street
Original address Via Oriani
Architect unknown
Date late 1930s
Map reference F5/G5

Located in the modern suburbs outside the city centre, towards Campo Polo, these are two good examples of the larger types of villa constructed towards the end of the 1930s for the wealthier Italians then settling in Asmara. Their modern style is typical of the period in which they were constructed. Such villas, with surrounding gardens, are common throughout Asmara. Being two storeys high, they conformed to the new building regulations imposed at the end of the 1930s. The distinctive buttress on the villa to the south is unlikely to be purely decorative and might in fact house a water tank.

MODERN VILLAS

Original function villas
Current address various
Original address various
Architect various
Date late 1930s
Map reference various

In the late 1930s, as Asmara grew and thousands of Italians arrived in the hope of settling there, the demand for housing often outstripped supply. Much of the housing built at this time was designed to provide for the lower classes of Italian immigrants, such as labourers and artisans, and therefore was modest in size and scale. Entirely new suburbs were planned, and hundreds of small villas designed and constructed. The architectural styles were varied, but certain trends are evident. Early villas (see pages 115-17) show a penchant for references to historic European styles, such as the Gothic and others from the medieval period. During the late 1930s, however, modern Rationalist forms deliberately lacking traditional decorative motifs that seemed to hark back to bygone ages were preferred. This spirit of modernity was reflected in both the overall style and the layout of the internal spaces.

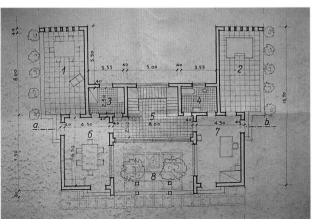

This selection of small villas illustrates the late 1930s Modernist style. It is difficult to assess exactly how many such buildings were constructed, as they have often been subjected to considerable alteration over the years, and although the designs for them suggest large and imposing structures they are in fact small and unassuming, which makes it difficult to locate and identify those that remain intact.

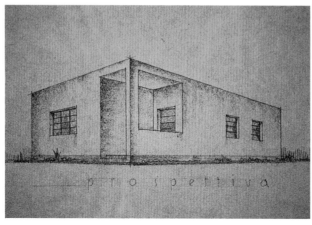

BUNGALOWS

Original function small villas
Current address various
Original address suburbs
Architect various
Date late 1930s
Map reference various

A small, compact type of residence similar to the villas mentioned above was also popular in Asmara in the late 1930s. These single-storey *villini* provided accommodation for small families or for individuals in the new suburban areas, particularly Gheza Banda, Gejeret and Godaif. Without any elaborate decoration, and contained within a small parcel of land, these houses provided sufficient living and garden space for one or two persons. They therefore became popular forms of housing for Italians with little money and few, if any, dependants.

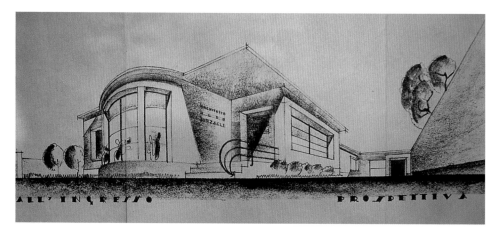

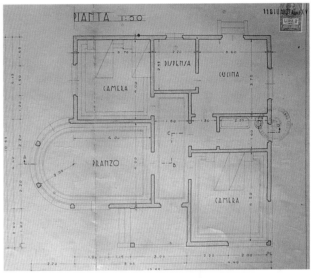

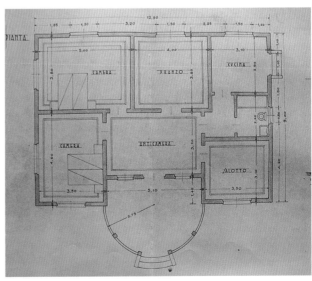

199

1941–52

MUNICIPALITY

Original function municipality
Current address Harnet Avenue
Original address Corso Italia
Architect unknown
Date 1951–71
Map reference D11/E11

The Municipality of Asmara was housed in a villa in the former European quarter until the late 1930s, and in a larger building on Denden Street, next to the Capitol Cinema, during the British Military Administration, but this is by far the most impressive and significant building that the municipality has occupied. Little is known about its early evolution. Planned during the late 1930s, this monumental two-storey building was constructed from the 1950s on a large area of land originally intended as a park at the southern end of Ad Ebrihim (the former Largo Puglie). The first stage of construction included a basement, a ground floor and a first floor, in the centre of which rose the instantly recognizable tower with a ceremonial balcony for public addresses, though it is doubtful that it was ever used for such a purpose. An official state assembly hall (see page 204, right) in the rear of the building was inaugurated by Queen Elizabeth II in 1965. In 1971 a third storey was added and the tower therefore heightened. With a third floor, and a newly extended tower forming a distinctive landmark, the enlarged building was a truly imposing structure.

Steps lead from the street to the main entrance, and a staircase continues inside the lobby up to the assembly hall and upper floors. On the exterior the windows in the upper two storeys are elongated, as opposed to those on the ground floor, which are squatter and almost square in form. The building is faced with random patterned green mosaic tiles, with window frames and sills made from grey marble. Recent renovation has involved the replacement of all the old rotten wooden window frames with newly fabricated ones.

SEMAETAT SECONDARY SCHOOL

Original name Convento e Collegio di Santa Anna
Current address Gurieto Street/Bada Street
Original address Via Dominicus/Via Regionaldo Giuliani
Architect unknown
Date 1947–56
Map reference H9

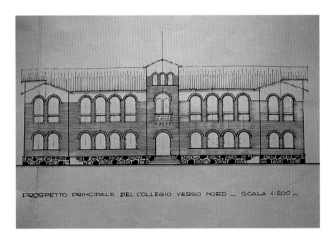

PROSPETTO PRINCIPALE DEL COLLEGIO VERSO NORD ~ SCALA 1:200 ~

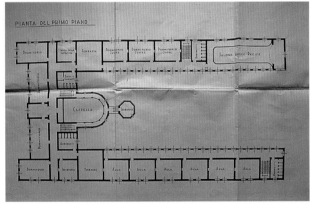

PIANTA DEL PRIMO PIANO

Located near the former railway crossing, this school was built in three stages. Foundations for the central section were laid on 7 December 1947, and it was finally completed on 25 October 1949. An Italian priest, Monsignor Marinoni, blessed the building on its opening. The west wing was constructed in 1952, followed by the east wing in 1956. The construction of these two wings provided a large inner courtyard, open at the southern end.

The style of the building has been influenced by Romanesque architecture, in particular the plain brick walls and the decorative details in the windows, such as stone mullions joined with round brick arches. Bricks have also been used to decorative effect in the entablature, as has painted plasterwork below the windows. Inside, there is little of note apart from some finely carved figures of angels on the main doorway inside the entrance hall. In 1982 the Ethiopian military régime under General Mengistu Hailemariam, the Dergue, expropriated all Catholic mission schools in Eritrea. The convent and its school were turned into a national secondary school, and it has remained as such ever since.

ASMARA SWIMMING POOL

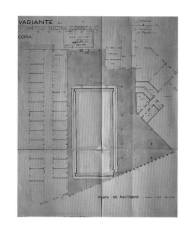

Original name Piscina Asmara
Current address 171-2 Street/Qohayto Street
Original address Via Bottego
Architect Arturo Mezzedimi
Date 1945
Map reference E7

The building for the Asmara swimming pool was one of the first major works by Arturo Mezzedimi, the renowned architect later favoured by Emperor Haile Selassie. It is designed in a distinctly modern style, with slender concrete frames providing an airy structure both externally and internally. The division of internal spaces allows for a bar and recreational area next to the swimming pool. With a wall of windows on the right of the entrance, in the bar area, and horizontal rows of skylights in the roof around the swimming pool, the interior receives abundant natural light. The rich colour scheme, including the use of turquoise paint throughout, and the differently coloured glass panes in the bar area give a naturally vibrant feel to the interior.

SHOPS AND APARTMENTS

Original name Palazzo Mutton
Current address Harnet Avenue/Ginda Street/Ad Ebrihim
Original address Corso Italia/Via Luciana/Largo Puglie
Architect Antonio Vitaliti
Date 1944
Map reference D11

The design of this commercial and residential building on Harnet Avenue, with its cantilevered upper balcony and rounded corners, is closely allied to that of Giuseppe Terragni's celebrated Novocomum apartment building in Como, Italy. Although it makes close reference to the Rationalist movement, by 1944 – its date of construction – this style would have been considered rather dated. The decision to take this approach might therefore have been fuelled more by nostalgia than political or professional allegiances.

The similarity of this building to Terragni's would be more evident if it had been finished. The original plan was for a six-storey building (top right), including the ground floor, but only the ground and first floors were completed. The original design would have dwarfed neighbouring buildings, including the fish and vegetable markets designed by Ferrazza and even the large high- court building constructed in the late 1930s on the opposite side of the road. An opening runs through the centre of the building to the rear – a feature not in the initial scheme; the curved corners on either side of this entrance were in the original proposal, where they rose to the full height of the building.

SHOPS AND APARTMENTS

Original function shops and apartments
Current address Nakfa Avenue/Ad Ebrihim
Original address Corso del Re/Largo Puglie
Architect Attilio Durisotti and Ferruccio Mazzanti
Date 1938; redeveloped 1946
Map reference D11

Situated next to the vegetable market, this imposing building has undergone many alterations yet has never been fully completed. An original small single-storey building was replaced in 1938 by a larger three-storey structure that formed the basis of the existing building, with two floors of apartments above shops at ground level. In 1946, however, an extensive redevelopment involved the partial addition of an extra floor and long, sweeping balconies, supported by slender pillars evocative of those on a cruise ship. The nautical theme was further underlined by the porthole windows at the south end of the west-facing wall. Unfinished supporting pillars at the east end of the north-facing wall provide evidence of the building's incompleteness. Unusually, external walkways rather than internal staircases and corridors provide access to the flats inside the courtyard.

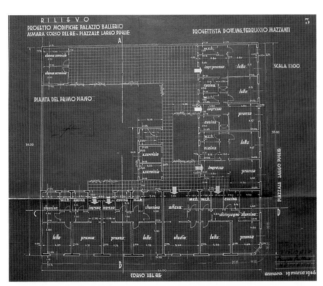

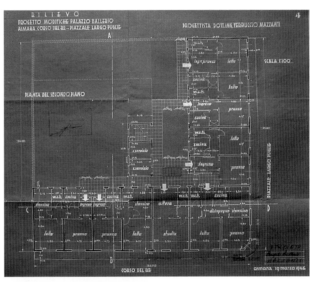

BRISTOL PENSION

Original function apartments
Current address 175-4 Street
Original address Via Giovanni Stella
Architect unknown
Date mid-1940s
Map reference E8

Constructed some time in the 1940s, the Bristol Pension is distinguished by its imposing and slightly projecting central stairwell column. It is peculiar that such a boldly symmetrical form was chosen for a sloping site, since the incline of the street contradicts the balance sought in the design. On the façade the second floor features a row of seven closely packed but evenly spaced windows on each side of the stairwell, while the first and ground floors each have only two on either side. The most notable interior feature is the floor, the top layer of which is made of finely ground small seashells, providing an incredibly smooth finish (right). The name Bristol Pension was given to the building in 1962 by the Eritrean owner, who had established a hotel of the same name in the former Italian brothel (see page 159) during the British Administration. The building was formerly an apartment block.

SHOPS AND APARTMENTS

Original function apartments (site of the Unione Militare)
Current address Nakfa Avenue/175-11 Street
Original address Corso del Re/Via Martini
Architect unknown
Date unknown
Map reference D8

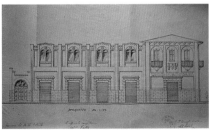

The site of this apartment building was once occupied by a medieval-style building housing the Military Union. The suggestion that this building was destroyed in 1941 by British aerial bombardment might be true – few buildings in Asmara were demolished deliberately because there was often enough space to build elsewhere. The building that replaced the older block is composed of a peculiar mixture of elements. The impression of solidity created by the use of concrete in construction and bold angular forms is at variance with the curved form of the structure and the gradient of the street on which it has been built. Nonetheless, it remains a distinctive building that provides a good standard of accommodation.

SHOPS AND APARTMENTS

Original function shops and apartments
Current address Selam Street/Akeleguzay Street
Original address Via Piemonte
Architect unknown
Date unknown
Map reference C10

A good example of Novecento styling, this block has a remarkably idiosyncratic façade, the most significant features of which include the brick balconies and columns of windows, and the rounded corner incorporating three round arches divided by simplified mullions. The design of the last element is similar to that of the Novecento-styled building on the north end of 175-11 Street (see page 186).

The elaborate interior fittings, including wooden banisters on iron railings, arched entrances to the apartments and fan-shaped windows, suggest that the building was constructed in the early 1940s or even late 1930s, though the date cannot be confirmed. Buildings in Asmara constructed after the 1940s tend not to have such detailing. Inside the apartments, the bathrooms have been designed with curious features, such as two arched cubicles containing a shower and a lavatory flanking the bath in the centre.

SHOPS AND APARTMENTS

Original function shops and apartments
Current address Segeneyti Street/Afabet Street
Original address Viale Badoglio/Via Milano
Architect Bruno Sclafani
Date 1942
Map reference B8

Located at the northern end of the former Mai Bela River, before it turned towards the south-west, this building projecting from the corner of the block has a rounded façade appropriate for the site on which it was built. On the façade a row of tightly packed, small rectangular windows denoting the first floor is enveloped by a slender concrete frame, at both ends of which are stucco mouldings of elephants. A series of more widely spaced windows down both sides of the building continue the horizontal alignment. Ground-floor doorways are vertically aligned with these windows, except on the corner façade where the entrance is divided into three parts. In 1939 a garage, much more modern in its styling, was proposed for this site (bottom left); it was never erected, and a further three years passed before a suitable building was constructed.

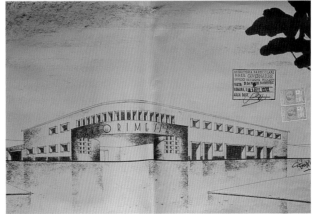

SHOPS AND APARTMENTS

Original function shops and apartments
Current address 176-9 Street/176-2 Street
Original address Via Carrara/Via Carbonara
Architect A. Bibolotti
Date 1944
Map reference E10

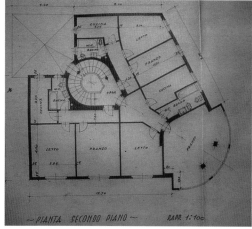

Positioned just south of Harnet Avenue, directly in line with the cathedral, this small commercial and residential building occupies a corner of a block. Like so many buildings in Asmara, it utilizes a rounded frontage to good effect as an aesthetically straightforward solution to the problem of a potentially irregular floor plan. The projecting balconies rounding the corner provide additional space and enhance the appearance of the building. Inside, the architect has maximized space by inserting a concrete spiral staircase that provides access to the upper floors.

VILLA GRAZIA

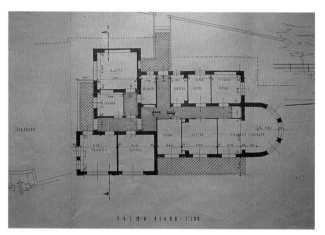

Original name Villa Grazia
Current address 173-10 Street
Original address Via Pennazzi
Architect Antonio Vitaliti
Date 1942
Map reference F10

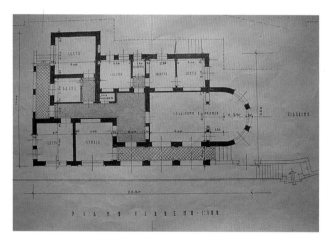

Positioned at the foot of the hill from which Ras Alula's fort commanded the Plain of Asmara, this was the second villa proposed for this site in two years. The building is clearly visible above the perimeter wall, with its bright red arched portico on display to the street. Access to the house is from the front, side and rear. The dramatic rounded northern face, incorporating one bedroom and the living room, with good views over the plain, maximizes the availability of natural light; the building's situation at the base of the eastern side of a steep hill means that it is illuminated by sunlight only in the mornings and early afternoons. Such large villas were not constructed after the 1940s, since the demand for them following Eritrea's federation with Ethiopia in 1952 waned with the departure of much of the expatriate community and the decline in the economy. Instead, single-storey accommodation became popular again.

'RUSTIC' VILLAS

Original function villas
Current address various
Original address various
Architect Roberto Cappellano
Date early 1940s
Map reference various

These 'rustic' villas, of which a large number were built in the early 1940s, demonstrate an important shift in the style of villa residences built in Asmara after the defeat of the Italians in 1941. After that date very few overtly modern ones were designed or constructed, and instead there was a reversion to traditional forms and references to vernacular and rural styles of architecture. As was mentioned in the introduction, the humiliation of defeat and the loss of their empire early in the Second World War might have triggered a backlash among Italians against symbolic references to the ideologies that thrust Italy towards war in the first place. The blatant modernity of Rationalism and other architectural styles of the 1930s might have appeared to lack obvious allusions to the motherland for which so many Italians in Eritrea no doubt yearned during this period of their decline in Africa.

One architect in particular, Roberto Cappellano, capitalized on the demand for more traditional architecture by designing and building many rustically styled cottages during the early 1940s. Evoking an idyllic vision of Italian rural life, these small buildings featured elements from Italian vernacular architecture such as the aedicule, the terracotta tiled roof and the decorative stonework used in the construction of the walls. Other villas designed during this period referred to traditional architecture in different ways, for example in the use of Romanesque features or the form of an Alpine chalet.

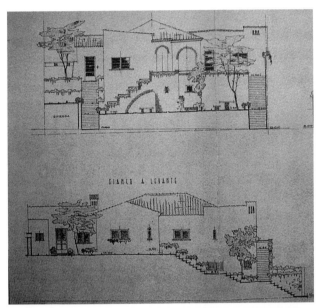

1952–91

THEOLOGICAL SCHOOL

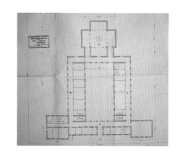

Original function Catholic seminary
Current address Maryam Gmbi Street
Original address Menelik II Avenue
Architect Lodovico Marchesi and Aniello Raffone
Date 1954
Map reference F5/F6

The adoption of both Orthodox and Catholic styles of architecture in this theological school makes it one of the more interesting of Asmara's many religious institutions. Of particular note are the courtyard and the large dome in the chapel. The courtyard is encircled by the classrooms and corridor, and the chapel at the back of the compound, forming the eastern side of the courtyard, is beautifully adorned with fine paintings and frescoes. The interior of the dome is perhaps the most striking feature – painted in gold and yellow, and perforated with twelve evenly spaced skylights. Between each of the four arches that support the dome are frescoes depicting religious figures, while around the base of the dome is a series of texts in Tigrinya script (opposite). The building has a surprisingly bland exterior, its façade being composed of a series of recessed arches in which are set the ground- and first-floor windows. The optimistic design drawing shows a vast open piazza in front of the school, though in fact a main road runs along there.

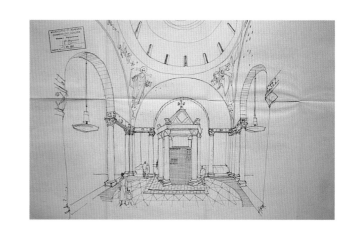

223

SHOPS AND APARTMENTS

Original name Palazzo Bahobesci
Current address Harnet Avenue/Fenql Street
Original address Haile Selassie I Avenue/Via Leonardo da Vinci
Architect Mario Fanano and Arturo Mezzedimi
Date 1955
Map reference D12

By the mid-1950s, Harnet Avenue had been extended to its present length. This apartment building, on the south-east corner of the street, was designed by the well-known architect Mezzedimi, in partnership with Fanano, for the renowned businessman Ahmed Ubed Bahobesci. However, financing the construction of this building drove Bahobesci to bankruptcy from which, it is alleged, he was never able to recover. This sizeable building, six storeys high, dominates the eastern end of Harnet Avenue before the road turns into the wastelands of Bahti Meskerem Square. With shops on the ground floor and apartments on the five floors above, the building remains one of Asmara's largest residential blocks.

SHOPS AND APARTMENTS

Original function shops and apartments
Current address Harnet Avenue/176-21 Street
Original address Haile Selassie I Avenue/Via Lorenzini
Architect Mario Fanano and Arturo Mezzedimi
Date 1956; 1958
Map reference D11

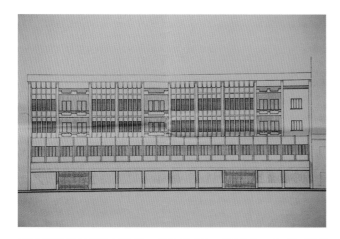

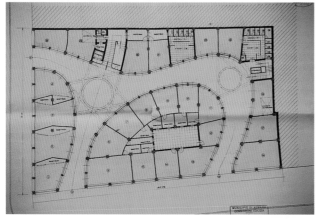

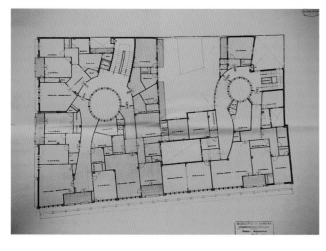

Although Harnet Avenue appears relatively densely built up today, its evolution occurred over most of the twentieth century, starting at the western end and extending eastwards. In the 1950s several buildings were proposed for Asmara's main thoroughfare, but the most imposing, again designed by the Fanano/Mezzedimi partnership for Ahmed Ubed Bahobesci, was never constructed. It would have consisted of a relatively small two-storey structure on the street front, with a towering twelve-storey apartment block (top right) behind it. Such an enormous structure in the heart of the city would have irreversibly altered the character of the city centre, and perhaps on those grounds it was refused planning permission, though financial problems are the far more likely explanation.

Two years later the same architects submitted a different proposal for the same plot, but for a different owner – Shoa Banin, an Asmarino Jew. At five storeys high, the new design was a little more sensitive to its surroundings and was the same height as the neighbouring buildings on both sides of the street. This complex has a highly irregular internal layout. On the ground floor an arcade passes through the building, with two entrances on Harnet Avenue and one on the side street. The junction between these three routes has been so arranged that the supporting iron girders are shaped in the form of the Star of David.

HIGH-RISE BUILDINGS

Original function high-rise buildings
Current address various
Original address various
Architect various
Date various
Map reference various

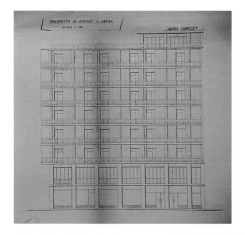

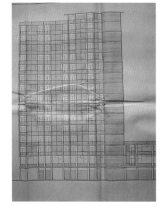

Following the international trend for high-rise buildings in the 1960s and 1970s, numerous tall buildings were proposed for Asmara, but few were built – probably owing to the economic and political instability of the country at this time. One example is the design for an eleven-storey building by Umberto di Mauro for the market square, submitted in 1966 (bottom, far right). Another was a second tower for the Nyala Hotel on Sematat Avenue (bottom, far left). Proposed in 1971, this colossal sixteen-storey tower would have been Asmara's tallest building, dwarfing its nine-storey neighbour (top left and bottom left). Construction of this tower did begin, but after the first three storeys work ceased and never resumed. One high-rise building that did get planning approval is the Ambassador Hotel opposite the Catholic cathedral, designed in 1972 by Alfredo Derde. The building of this odious structure in such a historic location was highly insensitive (top right and bottom right). The only positive point that can be made about such a building is that it provides a salient reminder of how just one act of unconcerned planning or design can so easily destroy the delicate fabric of an urban space.

SHOPS AND APARTMENTS

Original name Palazzo Amoroso
Current address Harnet Avenue/Mata Street
Original address Haile Selassie I Avenue/Via Dalmazia
Architect Arturo Mezzedimi
Date 1956
Map reference D11/E11

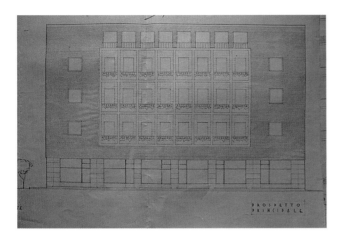

Originally designed in 1941 by the architect Giuseppe Malaguti, this large complex of apartments and shops was strongly influenced by Rationalist architecture in its bold simplicity. It appears that the project was shelved, perhaps owing to the Italian surrender, but it was later taken up by Mezzedimi. In 1941 smaller residential buildings were planned for the area to the rear of this building, but were never constructed.

The distinctive tiles in two shades of green, and the simple detailing of windows and recessed balconies, provide an uncluttered and attractive appearance to the façade on the former Viale Mussolini, which by the mid-1950s had been renamed Haile Selassie I Avenue. Now largely concealed by palm trees, the façade comprises a concrete frame divided into three rows and eight columns, providing each of the twenty-four windows with a single balcony.

The building occupies the space once covered by a park that was to form the end of Ferrazza's grand piazza extending from the north of the city (though the municipality building was later constructed on the piazza). Beyond this, to the east, were small commercial buildings, a printing press and the large building used as the High Court from the period of the British Administration to the present day.

APARTMENTS

Original function apartments
Current address Abdrbabu Street
Original address Via Generale Giardino/Via Puccini
Architect Mario Fanano and Arturo Mezzedimi
Date 1956
Map reference G10

One of the relatively few apartment blocks of this size to be built in Asmara after the end of the Italian administration, this rather eccentric building has clearly adopted certain stylistic references from Italian colonial architecture in the city. The tower on the right-hand side of the building, with decorative plasterwork depicting a panther or wildcat, dominates the asymmetrical façade. Owing to the incline on which the building stands, the entrance is raised slightly above ground level by a large flight of steps. Vertical alignment of the windows and doors is maintained throughout the exterior, while banding of different surface finishes aligns the windows horizontally. This banding is reversed between the main body of the building and its tower.

The reference to the panther is continued in the flooring on the internal staircase, and rustic images in stucco of farmers gathering their harvests of wheat and grapes adorn the walls and ceiling.

VILLAS

Original function villas
Current address various
Original address various
Architect various
Date early 1960s
Map reference various

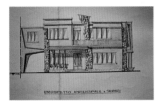

Following the annexation of Eritrea by Ethiopia in 1962, Haile Selassie's government set about building many new villas to replace the old workers' cottages from the 1930s. Consequently, Asmara's suburbs, particularly in the south, in and around the present suburb of Tiravolo, were expanded considerably.

This wave of construction gave rise to a particular style of villa, easily recognizable as a building of the early 1960s. The origins of this style are unknown, but it is characterized by the use of triangles and diagonal lines, almost chaotically arranged in direct (and perhaps deliberate) opposition to the strict vertical and horizontal alignment employed in many of the Italian buildings of the late 1930s. Many architects adopted this style, including Camillo Dionisio, Augusto Alfano and Bruno Mazzetti.

VILLAS

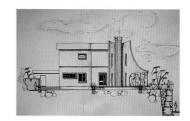

Original function villas
Current address various
Original address various
Architect various
Date early 1970s
Map reference various

A second wave of building of villas with their own distinctive style began in the early 1970s, after several years in which there had been a lull in construction in Asmara. Though nowhere near as numerous as their 1960s predecessors, the villas designed in the 1970s illustrate a distinctive modernization in living conditions, with garages, television aerials *etc*. At this time architects and engineers from Ethiopia, such as Tesfamariam Ogbi and Mikael Abraha, began to practise in Asmara, alongside such other experienced engineers as Alfredo Derde. However, very little construction took place in Asmara after Haile Selassie was deposed in 1974.

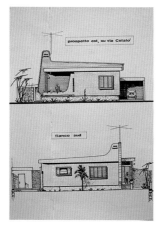

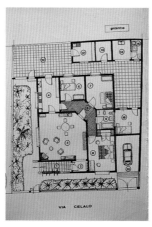

BAHTI MESKEREM SQUARE

Original name Red Square
Current address Bahti Meskerem Square/Harnet Avenue
Original address Red Square/National Avenue
Architect unknown
Date late 1930s–early 1980s
Map reference D12/D13

Perhaps the only significant structure to have been built during the Communist Dergue régime is that now known as Bahti Meskerem Square. At the eastern end of Harnet Avenue, the square was constructed on the site of the dismantled railway and was intended as a vast parade ground for the military under the command of the then Ethiopian leader, Mengistu. At that time the road was called National Avenue (the fourth name for this central thoroughfare in as many decades). Only one side of the arena was constructed; the second, larger half was never completed, though the piles for its supports were laid. What remains, then, is a vast, monstrous structure of grey-brown concrete occupying a significant portion of Asmara's city centre.

The square is used, however, for national celebrations and other gatherings, and as such it will no doubt remain a testament to one of the darkest periods of Eritrea's history before independence in 1991, when infrastructure and buildings were left to rot, and the people of Asmara suffered appalling oppression.

CHRONOLOGY

6000 BC Earliest cave paintings in Eritrea.

2500–1500 BC Egyptian traders visit the Eritrean coast.

800–400 BC First settled communities on the Plain of Asmara.

1st–7th centuries AD Rise and decline of the Axumite Empire.

338–39 Christianity introduced to Eritrea by Abuna Salama Kasate Berhan, from Tyre, Lebanon.

615 The First Exodus (*Sahaaba*) of the followers of the Prophet Mohammed to Eritrea, leading to the introduction of Islam there.

1520–26 Portuguese expeditions arrive in Eritrea.

1578 Amhara forces defeat Bahr Negash Yishak and the Turks to take control of the highlands.

1769 The Scottish explorer James Bruce crosses Eritrea *en route* to Ethiopia.

1813–23 The Egyptians occupy Massawa and the western lowlands.

1866 The local ruler, Bahr Negash Zeray, establishes his base in Asmara.

1868 British Napier expedition arrives on the Eritrean coast at Zula.

1869 In November the monk Giuseppe Sapeto purchases eighteen square kilometres (seven square miles) of land in Assab on behalf of the Rubattino Shipping Company, marking the official start of Italy's presence in Eritrea.

1875 In November Ras Wolde-Michael Solomon and the Tigrayans defeat the Egyptians at the Battle of Gundet.

1876 In March Ras Wolde-Michael Solomon and the Tigrayans defeat the Egyptians at the Battle of Gurae.

1878 In March Ras Wolde-Michael Solomon defeats the Tigrayan commander Ras Bayru in a battle in Asmara.

1879–80 The Rubattino Shipping Company purchases more land in Assab.

1879 In September Ras Wolde-Michael Solomon is betrayed by Ras Alula, mediator on behalf of Emperor Yohannes of Tigray, and imprisoned in Adua.

1882 The Italian government purchases the land owned by the Rubattino Shipping Company and administers Assab directly.

1885 The Italians are handed control of Massawa on 5 February.

1887 Ras Alula defeats the Italians at Dogali on 26 June.

1889 Emperor Yohannes is killed at the Battle of Matama in March.

1889 In May Emperor Menelik signs the Treaty of Uccialli with the Italians, resulting in the delineation of a border between Eritrea and Ethiopia.

1889 The Italians occupy the city of Keren on 2 June.

1889 The Italians take control of Asmara on 3 August.

1890 Official declaration of the state of Eritrea by Umberto I, King of Italy, on 1 January.

1893 Law defining extent of agricultural settlement is passed on 9 January.

1894 Uprising of the Eritrean population, led by Bahta Hagos, against the Italians on 14 December.

1896 Italians defeated at the Battle of Adua on 1 March.

1897 Ferdinando Martini appointed the first civilian Governor of Eritrea.

1900 Capital of Eritrea moved from Massawa to Asmara.

1902 International Exhibition of Modern Decorative Art held in Turin, Italy.

1902 First plans for the development of Asmara's central district.

1907 Giuseppe Salvago Raggi appointed Governor of Eritrea. His tenure of office ends in 1915.

1907 The first Eritrean military contingent involved in the Somalian campaign.

1908 Revoking of 1902 urban plans for Asmara, and submission of a new plan based on the creation of zones along racial lines.

1909 The artist Filippo Tommaso Marinetti publishes his *Manifeste du futurisme* ('Futurist Manifesto').

1911 Completion of the extension of the railway from Massawa to Asmara.

1912–32 Over 60,000 *askari* (indigenous soldiers) sent to fight in Libya.

1913 Odoardo Cavagnari presents his first master plan for Asmara.

1914 The Italian architect Antonio Sant'Elia publishes his *Manifesto dell'architettura futurista* ('Manifesto of Futurist Architecture').

1916 Odoardo Cavagnari submits revised designs of his 1913 master plan that delineate the four zones of Asmara: 'European', 'mixed', 'industrial' and 'native'.

1921 Earthquake devastates the port city of Massawa.

1921 Emergence of the Novecento movement in architecture in Italy.

1922 Mussolini comes to power in Italy on 29 October.

1922 Extension of the railway from Massawa to Keren.

1923 The architect Le Corbusier publishes his *Vers une architecture* ('Towards a New Architecture').

1923 Ethiopia becomes a member of the League of Nations on 13 October.

1925 The German architect Walter Gropius publishes his *Internationale Architektur*.

1930s Emergence of the Rationalist movement in Italian architecture.

1932 King Vittorio Emmanuele III of Italy visits Eritrea in October.

1933 Decree by the Italians for the expansion and development of the European zone of Asmara.

1935 The Italians invade Ethiopia on 3 October.

1937 Cable-car line between Asmara and Massawa completed in March.

1937 Announcement on 24 July of a competition for the master plan of Asmara.

1938 Implementation of strict laws on segregation of the races.

1938 Vittorio Cafiero submits his design for a master plan for Asmara.

1940 First aerial bombardment of Asmara by Allied air forces on 11 June.

1941 The Battle of Keren, between the Italians and the British, from 3 February to 27 March.

1941 British forces occupy Asmara on 1 April.

1941 The Mahaber Feqri Hager, the first political movement for Eritrean independence, formed on 5 May. In 1947 it becomes the Unionist Party, calling for "Eritrea with Ethiopia, One Ethiopia".

1941–52 The British administer Eritrea.

1946 The Moslem League is formed on 4 December.

1947 Launch on 18 February of the Liberal Progressive Party, demanding "Eritrea for Eritreans".

1947 Pro-Italian New Eritrea Party is established on 29 September.

1947 In November the Moslem League and the Liberal Progressive Party unite to form the Liberal League, calling for a British 'caretaker' government under the control of the United Nations (UN).

1949 In June the Eritrean political parties unite and found the Eritrean Independence Bloc.

1950 On 2 September the UN passes the United States-supported Resolution 390A(V) to create the federation of Ethiopia and Eritrea.

1952 Official declaration of the federation of Ethiopia and Eritrea on 11 September.

1953 On 22 May the United States signs a twenty-five-year lease of land in Asmara for a military base: Kagnew Station.

1958 Eritrean Liberation Movement (ELM) formed in Port Sudan. Flying of the Eritrean flag on government offices and other public buildings officially banned on 24 December.

1960 Eritrean Liberation Front (ELF) formed in Cairo on 10 July.

1960 Amharic declared the official language of Eritrea in September.

1961 On 1 September, on Mount Adal, Hamd Idris Awate fires the first shots of the armed struggle for Eritrean independence.

1961 In November ELF begins a military campaign in the western lowlands.

1962 The dissolution of the federation and annexation of Eritrea by Ethiopia, making Eritrea the fourteenth province of Ethiopia, on 14 November.

1970 People's Liberation Front (PLF) formed.

1970 Ethiopian forces kill over 600 civilians in the village of Ona on 1 December.

1971–74 Civil war between PLF and ELF.

1972 Anti-Ethiopian student demonstrations lead to closure of Eritrean schools in September.

1972 ELF–PLF (Eritrean Liberation Forces – People's Liberation Forces) formed in Beirut.

1974 Emperor Haile Selassie of Ethiopia overthrown on 12 September by a military coup, and a Marxist military régime, known as the Dergue and led by Mengistu Hailemariam, established in Ethiopia. Ethiopian *afegn* death squads patrol Asmara.

1975 Military régime in Ethiopia instigates brutal repression of Eritreans. Martial law implemented throughout the country. Thousands of civilians massacred, and hundreds of thousands flee to Sudan.

1977 PLF changes its name to EPLF at the First Congress, 23–31 January. EPLF liberates northern towns in Eritrea, including Keren and mainland Massawa.

1977–late 1980s Massive Soviet support for the Ethiopian régime.

1978 Forces for liberation occupy almost all Eritrea, except Asmara.

1978 EPLF forced into 'strategic withdrawal' to Sahel Mountains in northern Eritrea in November.

1978–88 EPLF camped in northern town of Nakfa.

1980–81 Civil war between EPLF and ELF.

1984–89 Catastrophic famine in Eritrea and northern Ethiopia. Over half a million Eritrean civilians displaced by war and nearly two million threatened by starvation.

1988 EPLF breaks out of Nakfa and routs Ethiopian forces in northern and western Eritrea.

1990 EPLF liberates the port city of Massawa on 10 February.

1991 EPLF forces liberate Asmara on 24 May.

1993 Referendum on independence conducted 23–25 April in Eritrea and among Eritrean emigrants; 99.8% vote for an independent state.

1993 Eritrea celebrates its official declaration of independence on 24 May.

1993 Eritrea becomes the 182nd member of the UN on 28 May.

1994 In February EPLF formally disbands and becomes the People's Front for Democracy and Justice (PFDJ).

1997 Eritrea launches its own currency, the *nakfa*, in November.

1998 Declaration of war on Eritrea by Ethiopian parliament on 13 May.

June 2000 Cessation of hostilities between Eritrea and Ethiopia.

2002–03 Official border demarcation between Eritrea and Ethiopia conducted by the UN.

2003 Failed rains in 2002 cause widespread famine throughout Eritrea.

2003 In May Eritrea celebrates its tenth anniversary as an independent state.

BIBLIOGRAPHY

M. Affron and M. Antliff (eds.), *Fascist Visions – Art and Ideology in France and Italy*, Princeton NJ (Princeton University Press) 1997

R. Banham, 'Futurism and Modern Architecture', *RIBA Journal*, LXIV, February 1957, pp. 129–39

P.M. Bardi, *Rapporto sull'architettura (per Mussolini)*, Rome (Polemiche – Edizioni di Critica Facista) 1931

J.S. Barnes, *The Universal Aspects of Fascism*, 2nd edn, London 1929

G. Barrera, 'The Construction of Racial Hierarchies in Colonial Eritrea: The Liberal and Early Fascist Period, 1897–1934', in *A Place in the Sun: Africa in Italian Africa in Italian Colonial Culture*, ed. P. Palumbo, Berkeley CA and Los Angeles (University of California Press) 2003

C.F. Beckingham, 'Some Records of Ethiopia 1593–1646', in *Works issued by the Hakluyt Society*, series 2, no. 107, London 1954

L. Benevolo, *History of Modern Architecture*, Cambridge MA (The MIT Press) 1971, II

L.V. Bertarelli, *Possedimenti e colonie, Isole Egee, Tripolitania, Cirenáica, Eritréa, Somália*, Milan (Guida d'Italia del Touring Club Italiano) 1929

A. Bizzoni, *L'Eritrea – nel passato e nel presente*, Milan (Società Editrice Sonzogno) 1897

C. Bordoni, *Cultura e propaganda nell'Italia fascista*, Florence (Messina) 1974

G. Branchi, *Missione in Abissinia 1883*, Rome (Tipografia di Gabinetto del Ministero degli Affari Esteri) 1889

P.V. Cannistraro (ed.), *Historical Dictionary of Fascist Italy*, Westport CT and London (Greenwood Publishing Group) 1982

V. Castellano, 'La populazione italiana dell'Eritrea dell 1924 al 1940', *Rivista italiana di demografia e statistica*, I, no. 4, 1948, p. 539

M. Castells, *The Information Age: Economy, Society and Culture, III: End of Millennium*, Oxford (Blackwell Publishers) 1998

L.F. Cogliati, *Tre anni in Eritrea*, Milan 1901

P. Collins, *Changing Ideas in Modern Architecture, 1750–1950*, London (McGill-Queens University Press) 1965

F. De Angelis, 'Il censimento del 1913 della popolazione italiana ed assimilata nella colonia Eritrea', *L'Africa Italiana. Bollettino della Società Africana d'Italia*, XXXX, 1921

A.J. De Grand, *Italian Fascism: its origin and development*, Lincoln (University of Nebraska) 1982

A. Del Boca, *The Ethiopian War: 1935–1941*, Chicago (University of Chicago Press) 1969

S. De Martino and A. Wall, *Cities of Childhood: Italian Colonies of the 1930s*, London (Architectural Association) 1988

E. Denison and E. Paice, *The Bradt Travel Guide to Eritrea*, 3rd edn, Chalfont St Peter, Bucks (Bradt Travel Guides) 2002

E. Denison and G.Y. Ren, 'The Evolutionary Development of Asmara – Colony to Hybridity', paper presented to the International Association for the Study of Traditional Environments (IASTE) biannual conference, Hong Kong, December 2002

R.A. Etlin, 'Italian Rationalism', *Progressive Architecture*, July 1983, pp. 86–94

R.A. Etlin, *Modernism in Italian Architecture 1890–1940*, Cambridge MA (The MIT Press) 1991

G. Fiore, *200 Pagine sull'Eritrea*, Asmara (Stabilimento Tipolitografico Percotto) 1952

K. Frampton, *Modern architecture: a critical history*, 2nd rev. edn, New York (W.W. Norton & Co.) 1985

J. Gargus (ed.), 'From Futurism to Rationalism: the Origins of Modern Italian Architecture', Architectural Design Profile 32, *Architectural Design*, LI, January–February 1981

M.D. Gaslini, *L'Italia sul Mar Rosso*, Milan (La Prora) 1938

D.Y. Ghirardo, 'Italian Architects and Fascist Politics: an Evaluation of the Rationalists' Role in Régime Building', *Journal of the Society of Architectural Historians*, XXXIX, May 1980, pp. 109–27

L. Goglia, *Storia fotografica dell'Impero fascista 1935–1941*, Rome-Bari (Editori Laterza) 1985

G. Gresleri, P.G. Massaretti and S. Zagnoni, *Architettura Italiana d'Oltremare, 1870–1940*, Venice (Marsilio) 1993

W. Gropius, *Internationale Architektur*, 2nd rev. edn, Munich 1925

Istituto Agricolo Coloniale, *Eritrea – Some Photographic Representations of Italy's Action*, Florence 1946

F. Keene (ed.), *Neither Liberty nor Bread: The Meaning and Tragedy of Fascism*, New York (Harper & Bros) 1940

M. Labó, *Giuseppe Terragni*, Milan (Il Balcone) 1947

R. Lamb, *Mussolini and the British*, London (John Murray) 1997

B. Lindahl, *Architectural History of Ethiopia in Pictures*, Addis Ababa (Artistic Printers) 1970

F. Locatelli, 'Urban Segregation and Definition of the Colonial Social Order: The Case of Prostitution in Asmara 1889–1941', paper presented to the First International Conference of Eritrean Studies, Asmara, July 2001

F. Martini, *Nell'Africa Italiana – impressione e ricordi*, Milan (Fratelli Treves) 1885

Y. Mesghenna, 'Italian Colonialism: A Case Study of Eritrea, 1869–1934: Motives, Praxis and Result', *Skrifter utgivna av Ekonomisk-historiska föreningen i Lund*, LVIII, 1988

P. Mezzanotte, 'La prima mostra d'architettura promossa dalla famiglia artistica di Milano', *Architettura e Arti Decorative*, I, September–October 1921, pp. 298–304

Ministero delle Colonie, *Ferrovia Massaua–Asmara*, Rome (Governo della colonia Eritrea, Stab. Danesi) 1914

M. Moretto, *Guida commerciale dell'A.O.I.*, Asmara (Tipografico Coloniale M. Fioretti) 1939

I.S. Munro, *Through Fascism to World Power: A History of the Revolution in Italy*, London (Gordon Press) 1933

B. Mussolini, *Fascism: Doctrines and Institutions*, New York (Howard Fertig) 1935

P. Oliver (ed.), *Shelter in Africa*, London (Barrie and Jenkins) 1971

E. Onnis, 'La città di Asmara', diss., Padua, Università degli Studi di Padova, 1956

E.S. Pankhurst, *Eritrea on the Eve*, Woodford Green, Essex, 1952

R. Pankhurst, *History of Ethiopian Towns from the Mid Nineteenth Century to 1935*, Stuttgart (Coronet Books) 1985

R. Paoli, *Nella colonia Eritrea*, Milan (Fratelli Treves) 1908

L. Pennazzi, *Dal Po ai due Nili – Massawa, Keren, Kassala*, Milan (Fratelli Treves) 1882

A. Pica, *Nuova architettura italiana*, Milan (Quaderni della Triennale) 1936

M. Pio-Giovanni, 'A proposito di Cassala', in *Tipografia della pace di Filippo Cuggiani*, Rome 1894

R. Plant, *Architecture of the Tigre, Ethiopia*, Worcester (Raven's Educational and Development Services Ltd) 1985

L. Preti, *Impero fascista: africani ed ebrei*, Milan (Mursia) 1968

F. Russell (ed.), *Art Nouveau Architecture*, New York (Outlet Books) 1986

A. Sartoris, *Introduzione alla architettura moderna*, 3rd rev. edn, Milan 1949

J. Schnapp, 'Epic Demonstrations: Fascist Modernity and the 1932 Exhibition of the Fascist Revolution', in *Fascism, Aesthetics and Culture*, ed. R.J. Golsan, Lebanon NH (University Press of New England) 1992, pp. 1–37

T. Sillani and E. De Bono, *L'Africa Orientale Italiana e il conflitto Italo-Etiopico*, Rome (La Rassegna Italiana) 1936

J. Summerson, *Heavenly Mansions and other Essays on Architecture*, New York (W.W. Norton & Co.) 1963, pp. 2, 23

E.R. Tannenbaum, *The Fascist Experience: Italian Society and Culture, 1922–1945*, London (Allen Lane) 1972

N. Tekeste, *Italian Colonialism in Eritrea, 1882–1941. Policies, Praxis and Impact*, Uppsala (Uppsala University) 1987

C. Tisdall and A. Bozzolla, *Futurism*, New York and Toronto (Thames & Hudson) 1985

G.K.N. Trevaskis, *Eritrea. A Colony in Transition: 1941–1952*, Oxford (Oxford University Press) 1960

J.S. Trimingham, *Islam in Ethiopia*, London (Frank Cass & Co.) 1962

United Nations Centre for Human Settlements, *An Urbanizing World: Global Report on Human Settlements 1996*, Oxford (Oxford University Press) 1996

United Nations Centre for Human Settlements, *Cities in a Globalizing World: Global Report on Human Settlements 2001*, London (Earthscan Publications) 2001

United Nations Economic Commission for Africa, *Rural Buildings in Africa and the World* (UNECA) 1970

PICTURE CREDITS

Archive images are from the following sources:

L'Africa Orientale, Milan (A. Mondadori) 1938: pp. 58 (right), 127 (top right), 145 (top right), 151 (top right), 154 (top right), 163 (top right), 172 (top right), 185 (top right), 188 (top right), 189 (top right)

Gli Annali dell'Africa Italiana, Rome (A. Mondadori) 1938, IV: p.54 (centre), 66 (right), 126 (top right), 129 (top right), 190 (top right), 194 (top right)

A. Bizzoni, *L'Eritrea – nel passato e nel presente*, Milan (Società Editrice Sonzogno) 1897: pp. 20 (right), 23, 26, 89 (top right), 90 (top right), 128 (top right)

L.F. Cogliati, *Tre anni in Eritrea*, Milan 1901: pp. 28, 32 (top left and bottom left), 110 (top right), 134 (top right)

S. De Martino and A. Wall, *Cities of Childhood: Italian Colonies of the 1930s*, London (Architectural Association) 1988: p. 49 (bottom)

Eritrea – Some Photographic Representations of Italy's Action, Florence (Istituto Agricolo Coloniale) 1946: pp. 25 (top), 29 (top left and bottom left), 33 (bottom)

L. Goglia, *Storia fotografica dell'Impero fascista 1935–1941*, Rome-Bari (Editori Laterza) 1985: pp. 48 (left), 54 (left)

Per gentile concessione dell'Istituto Italiano per l'Africa e l'Oriente: pp. 2, 25 (bottom), 30 (bottom), 36, 37, 38, 39, 40–41, 46–47, 53, 57, 58 (left), 60, 61 (bottom), 63 (right), 70, 97 (top right), 107 (bottom), 118 (top right), 143 (top right and bottom left), 148 (top right), 155 (top right)

Vahe Koroghlian: p. 35 (left)

F. Martini, *Nell'Africa Italiana – impressione e ricordi*, Milan (Fratelli Treves) 1885: p. 27

Municipality of Asmara: pp. 52, 54 (right), 55, 59, 61 (top), 62 (bottom), 64 (top right), 65, 66 (left), 67 (top left and top right), 72, 96 (top right), 99 (right and top right), 107 (top), 109 (top right), 117 (bottom right), 123, 129 (centre and centre right), 131 (top and bottom), 132 (left), 137 (centre), 138 (top right), 139 (top right), 141 (top right), 142, 143 (centre), 146 (top right), 147 (top right), 149 (top right), 151 (centre), 155 (bottom left and bottom right), 157 (bottom left and bottom right), 160 (top right, bottom left and bottom right), 161 (bottom left and bottom right), 162 (top), 163 (centre and bottom), 166 (top and left), 168 (top right), 170 (centre), 171, 172 (left), 174 (bottom left and top right), 175 (top right), 176 (top right), 177 (left and top right), 180 (top right), 181, 182 (top right), 183 (top right), 184 (top right), 186 (top right and bottom), 187 (top right), 188 (centre right and bottom), 189 (bottom left and bottom right), 191 (top right and bottom), 192 (top left, bottom left and top right), 193 (top right, centre right and bottom right), 195, 196, 197 (bottom), 198 (bottom), 199, 202 (bottom), 203 (top right and bottom), 205 (top left and bottom left), 206 (top right), 207 (top right), 209, 211 (bottom), 213 (top right and bottom), 214 (right), 215 (top), 216 (top right, centre left and centre right), 218, 219, 222 (top right, bottom left and bottom right), 223 (top right), 224 (bottom), 225 (top left, centre left, bottom left and top right), 226 (top left, top right, bottom far left and bottom far right), 227 (top right and left), 228 (top right), 229 (left), 230 (top right, bottom left and bottom right)

La Nuova Italia d'Oltremare 1, l'opera del fascismo nelle colonie italiane, Milan (A. Mondadori) 1938: p. 135 (top right)

Private Collections, Asmara: pp. 21, 43 (bottom), 48 (top), 64 (top left), 91 (top right), 92 (top right), 93 (top right), 94 (top right), 97 (bottom right), 98 (top right), 100 (top right), 101 (top right), 102 (top right), 111 (top right), 112 (top right), 113 (top right), 122 (top right), 124 (top right), 125 (top right), 130 (top right), 137 (top right), 150 (bottom), 157 (top right), 158 (top right), 169 (top right), 170 (top right), 178 (top right), 202 (top right), 211 (top right), 224 (top right)

Frà Ezio Tonini: p. 32 (right)

INDEX

SCHIZZO
PROSPETTICO

PROSPETTO

VEDUTA PROSP.